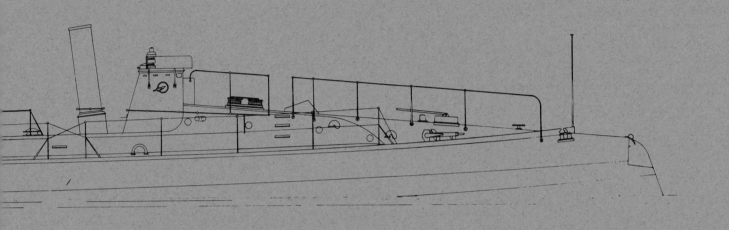

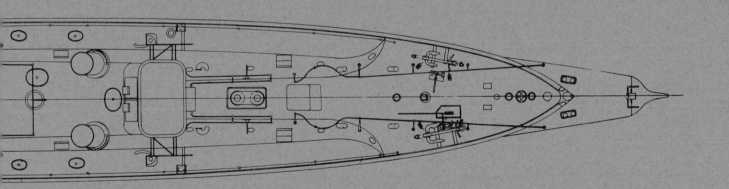

(front cover) E.W.Cooke's painting shows the *Devastation*, the first sea-going mastless battleship firing a Royal Salute from one of her 35-ton muzzle-loading rifled guns. She is dressed overall in honour of a royal visit. In the background are the royal yacht and several masted ironclads of the Channel Fleet.

(back cover) This painting of the Mediterranean Fleet in Grand Harbour, Malta, shows a spectrum of different Victorian warship types including the white-hulled box battery ship *Alexandra* (the flagship), the 'mastless' turret battleship *Dreadnought*, the immediate successor of the *Devastation* and *Thunderer*, the first examples of this type, and a seagoing masted turret ship, *Colossus*.

(front endpaper) Swedish torpedo-boat *Hugin*, 1884, built by Thornycroft.

(back endpaper) Design of 150-ton torpedo-boat for Spain, 1905, by Thornycroft.

© Crown copyright 1980
First published 1980

ISBN 0 11 290318 5

Design by HMSO Graphic Design

Printed in England for
Her Majesty's Stationery Office
by W. S. Cowell Ltd, Ipswich

Dd 596285   K160

National Maritime Museum

THE SHIP

Steam, Steel and Torpedoes

The Warship in the 19th Century

David Lyon

To Tom McGrath with regards

David J. Lyon

London
Her Majesty's Stationery Office

Contents

(below) Armstrong design for 6-pounder Hotchkiss quick-firing gun on automatic jacket recoil mounting.

Introduction by the General Editor

This is the eighth of a series of ten short books on the development of the ship, both the merchant vessel and the specialized vessel of war, from the earliest times to the present day, commissioned and produced jointly by The National Martime Museum and Her Majesty's Stationery Office.

The books are each self-contained, each dealing with one aspect of the subject, but together they cover the evolution of vessels in terms which are detailed, accurate and up-to-date. They incorporate the latest available information and the latest thinking on the subject, but they are readily intelligible to the interested non-specialist, professional historian or layman.

Above all, as should be expected from the only large and comprehensive general historical museum in the world which deals especially with the impact of the sea on the development of human culture and civilization, the approach is unromantic and realistic. Merchant ships were and are machines for carrying cargo profitably. They carried the trade and, in the words of the very distinguished author of the second book of the series, 'the creation of wealth through trade is at the root of political and military power'. The vessel of war, the maritime vehicle of that power, follows, and she is a machine for men to fight from or with.

It follows from such an approach that the illustrations to this series are for the most part from contemporary sources. The reader can form his own conclusions from the evidence, written and visual. We have not commissioned hypothetical reconstructions, the annotation of which, done properly, would take up much of the text.

In this book, Mr Lyon deals with the worldwide development of the warship in the Victorian era. Although the centre of his scene is in Britain, his approach, as with all the authors in this series, is international, for shipping and shipbuilding are international businesses in which developments in one country rapidly spread all over the world. Following the spirit of the series, he has related the development of the man-of-war to the general industrial advance of the period and he clearly shows how close the relationship was.

Navies in the 19th century, though then, as at all times, periodically starved of resources, were at times nevertheless able to innovate and initiate and bear development costs, so that the merchant shipping industry subsequently benefited. To give only two examples, though navies, for good reasons, were slow to adopt iron construction, and it was that remarkable pioneer merchant steamship, the *Great Britain*, now preserved at Bristol, which pioneered the way for big iron ships, the demand from the Navy in Britain for steel in shipbuilding quantities and qualities and sizes resulted in the product's availability at prices which made economically possible its rapid adoption for the construction of merchant ships. Similarly, naval construction pioneered the way for the adoption by passenger liners of propulsion by more than two screws.

Mr Lyon has been one of the members of the Staff of the National Maritime Museum looking after the great collection of engineering drawings of ships, by far the largest of its kind in the world, for many years. He is an established authority on the history of the construction of war vessels and their armament in the period he deals with in this book.

Basil Greenhill
DIRECTOR, NATIONAL MARITIME MUSEUM
General Editor

(below) Steam assists sail at the bombardment of Acre in 1841. The small paddle-steamers in the foreground proved useful auxiliaries to the sailing battleships, frigates and sloops which are still doing the main business of fighting in the background.

The background to 19th century warship development

During the 19th century rapid, drastic and continuous technical change became the accepted background of life for warship designers and users. In the first half of the century the adoption of steam propulsion and then iron construction began a process which accelerated in the second half of the century with improvements in guns, the adoption of armour, the invention of mines and torpedoes, the use of steel construction and of electricity. In 1800 there was a tradition of intermittent detailed change in warship design which did not alter fundamentals, but produced a gradual growth in performance and gunpower over the years. By 1900 it had become a truism that a new warship would become obsolete, if not totally useless, during the course of its service life.

Behind the radical changes in warship design which took place in this century lie the complex of technological, economic and social changes we label the 'Industrial Revolution'. Britain in the late 18th century was the setting for a series of often inter-related improvements in coalmining, iron founding, the textile industries and transportation, which began an accelerating process that made these islands into the world's first industrial nation. As the 19th century drew on these changes began to take place in Western Europe and North America as well. Britain's first place in industrialisation owed much to, and then contributed greatly towards, her position as the leading maritime nation, in both naval and mercantile spheres.

The increasing pace of industrialisation and of technical change was bound to influence warship design. In turn the demands of warship building had their own effect on industries. For example, the need for better armour and guns had profound effects on metallurgical techniques, whilst the immense requirements of navies for first iron then steel led to the creation of bigger foundries and rolling mills.

This background of technical and industrial change is vital to a full understanding of warship design. For example, the development of long-range gunnery techniques at the end of the century was dependent on the invention of new explosives and improvements in gun manufacture. Before these occurred it was not possible for guns to fire at ranges beyond those enshrined in the traditional 'three mile limit' of territorial waters. The new gunnery control methods would also lean heavily on newly developed hydraulic and electric engineering.

It is equally important to understand the influence of certain practical matters on the development of the warship. For example, the inefficiency and unreliability of early engines explain the reluctance of navies to do away with sails, and the unseaworthiness of early torpedo craft made them less effective in practice than in theory. Indeed, in an age which knows about the techniques of operational research and of the careful analysis of the purpose and achievements of weaponry, the later 19th century, in particular, too often seems to drift away from reality in its warship designs, in going for the highest possible trial speed or the largest possible gun without, by our standards, any real consideration of the merits of the case.

However, it must be remembered that there was little in the way of practical experience to guide the warship designers of the day, once the developments of the middle of the century had made irrelevant the experience of fighting under sail in the great maritime wars which ended in 1815. There were no major fleet actions at sea between major naval powers in the 90 years which lay between Trafalgar and Tsushima, battles which neatly delimit our period. There was an arguable exception in the Austrian victory over a technically superior but tactically inferior Italian force at Lissa (1866). Superior fleets destroyed inferior ones lying at anchor at Navarino (1827) and Sinope (1853), but there were few lessons here for designers. Much the same is true of most of the actions between small squadrons or individual ships before the 1850's.

The naval battles during the South American wars for independence, Portuguese civil war and the grossly unequal contests between British warships and Chinese junks during the opium wars with China did no more for the development of naval technology than did the rather more numerous shore bombardments of the period, starting with the bombardment of Algiers by an Anglo-Dutch squadron in 1816. Far

In the battle of Mobile Bay, 1864, the 'great rebel Iron Clad Ram *Tennessee*' is surrounded and overwhelmed by Federal warships. Conventional steam warships on the left of the picture are combined with one- and two-turret monitors, and there is a paddle merchantman in the background converted to a gunboat. The *Tennessee* is of the same 'floating battery' type with sloping sides as the earlier *Merrimac/Virginia*.

more important was the demonstration of the need to develop new weapons and techniques during the early contests between ship and shore during the Crimean War (1854-6). Possibly the most interesting ship action of the period before this attracted little attention then or later. This was the battle off Yucatan (1843) between two brigs of the Texas Navy and a Mexican squadron including two steamers, one of them built of iron. Here, shells were used by ships at sea against other ships for the first time, and the Texan sailing ships actually came off best.

After the Crimean War, as radical technical change became the order of the day, each new conflict involving warships was eagerly studied for indications of how new ships and weapons performed. The American Civil War (1861-5) was the biggest and longest naval war of the period, but the contestants were not evenly matched at sea, and the improvised warships which fought, most notably at Hampton Roads, did not compare particularly well with British or French contemporaries. Despite the vogue for Monitor-type vessels in the following years, probably the most important influence of this war on naval design was on the development of the torpedo-boat. Further impetus in this direction was provided by the Russian torpedo-boat successes against the Turks in 1877-8.

One ship, the British-built Peruvian turret ironclad *Huascar*, provided a great deal of information to the commentators, first, by an indecisive action with British unarmoured ships when she had temporarily turned pirate in 1877. This proved the efficacy of her armour. Later she fought in the 'War of the Pacific' (1879-81) when she was captured by the Chileans (who still preserve her). This and other South American wars and revolutions, the river war of the alliance against Paraguay, and the torpedo-boat actions during Brazilian and Chilean revolutions (when torpedoes were successfully used against battleships) gave few real clues about the way naval warfare and weapons should be developed.

In both the Sino-Japanese (1894-5) and Spanish American (1898-9) wars the sides were too unevenly balanced in training, efficiency, and, in the latter case, numbers, for many useful lessons to emerge. Even looking back with the advantage of hindsight it is difficult to imagine how major naval battles would have been fought, and how ships of the major navies would have performed against one another during the period of extreme technical change which began half way through the century. For example, despite the poor showing of French battleship designs manned by Russians against Japanese-manned British-built ships during the Russo-Japanese war (1904-5), it is difficult to be sure that the same results would have obtained had Britain and France gone to war over the Fashoda Incident at the end of the 1890's (though it seems possible that this might have been the case).

One thing that can be certain throughout the 19th century is that there was one country that was not only the strongest at sea in actuality, but also had a reserve of maritime strength, not obvious at first sight, which was to grow greater still. This was Britain, the leading naval power of the age. At the end of the Napoleonic Wars she had the largest and most effective navy and mercantile marine. As the effects of her lead in industrialisation began to take effect on new construction with the adoption of steam, iron hulls and so on, she assumed a lead in warship-building – if not necessarily in design – which she retained well into the 20th century. Not only did the British ship-building industry build all the warships needed for the Royal Navy, but from the 1820's it began supplying warships in numbers for other navies as well. From the 1860's Britain could be considered as shipbuilder to the world, both of warships and of merchant ships.

Never before or since has any one country held such a position of primacy in any one industry. France – for most of the century the nearest rival – could hardly compete either in number of yards, volume of production or speed of building. The French Navy could, as it did in the 1850's and 1870's, build up its strength to close that of Britain; but once the threat became apparent Britain had the reserves of shipbuilding strength to outdistance her rival with ease.

Perhaps the best example of this is the British reaction to the wooden-hulled ironclad *Gloire*. Instead of building a similar vessel the British laid down the *Warrior*, much larger, faster, and with an iron hull. Again, in the 1890's British battleships could be, and were, built in less than half the time taken by their French equivalents.

The combination of the largest navy and the greatest shipbuilding industry means that at some times in the second half of the century getting on for half the warships in the world were British-built. There is no doubt that Britain built far more warships (perhaps a third of the total) in the course of the century than any other nation. It seems, therefore, justifiable to write this book mainly from a British viewpoint, showing the development of the warship as it appears in the ships of the largest navy of the time, though taking into account the numerous important foreign developments, mainly through their effect on British design.

In any case the countries which played a major part in the development of warship design during the course of the century were few in number, and, apart from the USA, all European. The Japanese did

(left) The *Shah* in the foreground of the picture, and the corvette *Amethyst* astern of her, are kept from closing with the Peruvian *Huascar* on the right because of their lack of armour. Their guns, though inflicting considerable superficial damage on that small ironclad, do not defeat her.

(right) British shipbuilding. The massive *Sans Pareil*, a turret battleship whose turret was mounted forward, is seen just before her launch by the Thames Iron Works. The date is 1887. The *Sans Pareil*'s sister *Victoria* was to be lost in a famous collision.

not begin seriously designing major warships for themselves until they beat Russia. Even then they remained heavily influenced by British methods for some time.

The USA, although producing excellent sailing warship designs, and playing a leading role in the introduction of the steam warship, was gradually driven from the forefront of major warship design by the fact that its heavy industries could not compete with those of Britain and France during the ironclad era. This fact was disguised for a while by the interest and ingenuity of the Civil War improvisations, but after the end of that war both the navy and the shipbuilding industry stagnated. The revival in the late 1880's required at first a certain amount of foreign assistance in the form of large castings and other items obtained from Britain, but by then American industrial strength and skill were growing fast. By the end of the century not only was the American Navy quickly surpassing the French in

strength, but American warship designers were again producing original and interesting designs, owing little to foreign influence, for peculiarly American requirements.

Two newly united nations began to design their own warships by the 1870's. Italy, though relying heavily on British industrial help, produced some interesting, if extreme, designs such as the battleship *Duilio*. Germany, on the other hand, made a determined effort to build up her own shipbuilding and designing strength. Mainly thanks to her rapid growth in industrial power she succeeded very well. Her great achievements in battleship design did not come till after the *Dreadnought*, but by then she had already developed the light cruiser as a new kind of warship. In addition, one German shipbuilder, Schichau, had proved very successful in developing sturdy and seaworthy torpedo boats, which had sold well overseas.

Holland, Denmark and Sweden, though continuing to build the majority of their own warships and keeping up with modern developments, did little of general significance. Much the same could be said

The *Mainz* of 1909 shows one of the later stages in the evolution of the German light cruiser. The picture is by the great British expert on warships, Dr Oscar Parkes. By this time British light cruisers were not dissimilar in general appearance.

of the newer, but also efficient, Austrian Navy. The traditional naval powers of Iberia, Spain and Portugal, failing to industrialise to any great extent, tended to buy their warships from abroad.

The 'maverick' amongst the European naval powers was Russia. Though relying heavily on foreign industrial help and designs, the Russians produced some interesting and important developments, such as the first armoured cruiser. They also were responsible for some very odd ideas, of which the circular 'Popoffkas' are the best known (see page 52). Russia also played an important part in the early history of mine and torpedo warfare. Normally, however, performance failed to measure up to intent, as was cruelly revealed by the experience of the Russo-Japanese War.

During the last third of the 19th century, Russia's greatest ally was France, and that country provided a large proportion of her warship designs. France was the one state which throughout the century could be considered a serious rival to Britain in the naval sphere, but, as we have seen, was constantly let down by her slower industrialisation. French designers were consistently coming up with new developments; the first ironclad, the shell gun, the first use of steel in warship construction, the first superfiring gun (gun mounted above and behind another gun and firing over the top of it). Many of their designs were excellent, and were often built in sufficient numbers to produce naval 'scares' in Britain. It was never possible, however, to keep up enough momentum to surpass the British. Either the Royal Navy built more ships, or built them faster in an emergency. Alternatively, a French threat might be countered by an entirely new design, for example, the destroyer, which cancelled out French superiority in torpedo boats in the 1890's.

The French Navy also suffered from not being the country's most vital armed service. When the army was defeated in 1870 the navy was neglected in favour of building up land defences. In the 1880's more harm than good was done by the theories of the *Jeune École* (a group of French naval theorists) which emphasised the importance of torpedo boats and commerce-raiding cruisers for attacking the great maritime rival, Britain. In the early years of the 20th century, thanks to the combination of the Anglo-French *rapprochement* and the pernicious influence of a deplorable Minister of Marine, the French Navy entered a period of neglect and declined to a position of strength considerably less than that of either Germany or the USA.

The Royal Navy itself had its ups and down during the course of the 19th century, periods of slow decline with little new building being followed by 'scares' and heavy building programmes. In the 1840's the growing force of French steamships caused a fear of invasion, so the re-equipment of the navy with screw vessels was accelerated. The Crimean War caused a vast building programme of gunboats and other vessels for shore bombardment, one of the few occasions during the century when British industry really showed what it could do in a national emergency. Shortly afterwards, the appearance of the *Gloire* set in train the large ironclad programme of the 1860's. Prussia's defeat of France in 1870 resulted in a slackening of pressure and, in combination with Gladstonian economic theories of reducing public spending, led to the 'dark ages of the Victorian Navy'. Even during this low period, when there was no serious foreign challenge to British naval superiority, the Royal Navy's activities in ship design did not come to a halt, for this was when Britain took the lead in introducing the torpedo boat.

In the mid-1880's a Russian war scare began a very different era. Russia and France were allies, and together superior at sea to the Royal Navy, with both building more ships. The result was the massive re-equipment programme of the Naval Defence Act of 1889. From this time on the pace of naval rivalry grew ever greater, though by 1900 Germany was replacing France as the chief rival. Increasing fears of the inevitability of obsolescence caused by the increasing pace of technical change exacerbated the situation. Germany was conspicuously setting out to challenge Britain at sea, with diplomatic blackmail and eventual supremacy in mind. The conditions for the appearance of the *Dreadnought*, perhaps the most important case of the influence of warship design on history, had been prepared.

It is against this background of industry, politics, economics and diplomacy that we must consider the story of the development of the warship in the 19th century. Of course, in a short work there is no room to do more than pick up the outlines and detect the significant developments. This means singling out the ships which made the most important technical advances, thereby simplifying what is essentially a very detailed story. It is worth remembering that much warship development occurs by means of small improvements from one ship to the next, a slow, and sometimes almost imperceptible process.

The tiny *Diana* was the first British steam warship to see action, in the First Burma War of the mid-1820's. She was too small to carry guns, so when she was temporarily acquired for service during the war she was given an armament of Congreve Rockets, whose firing rails can be seen amidships. She proved very useful in support of the landings during this amphibious campaign.

Sail to steam

Though the first steam warship was launched in 1814 it was not until the middle of the century that sail ceased to be the only method of propulsion of major warships, and not until nearly the end of the century that it ceased to be fitted as an auxiliary to vessels designed for long cruises. The slowness of this change, so often blamed on unthinking conservatism (which did play its part), owes much to the deficiencies of early steam propulsion. We tend to look at the first half of the century through the wrong end of the telescope, our view influenced by the much more rapid pace of change afterwards. Obvious though it may be to us that steam should replace sail, it was less so in the 1820's and 1830's. Steam engines were extremely unreliable, very heavy for the small amount of power they produced, and extremely uneconomical in fuel.

The combination of unreliability and very short range would have been enough to cause second thoughts amongst the navies of the world. To this may be added the fact that the only workable method of propulsion for a seagoing steamer until the 1840's was the paddle wheel. The best position for this was on either side amidships, best, that is, from the point of view of positioning of weights, mechanical convenience and seaworthiness. However, it not only made the wheels very vulnerable to both weather and enemy fire, it also meant that fewer guns could be carried, and these not in the optimum positions. This was crucial at a time when the numbers of guns carried on the broadside were the measure of a warship's power. Less immediately obvious was that half-way along the hull was the least desirable position to obtain propulsive efficiency.

The greater reliability of sail and the gun-carrying ability of sailing warships meant that up till the 1840's it was only the smaller warships that were built as steamers. Their main function was as auxiliaries, and particularly as tugs, for the capital ships of the day, the sailing line of battle ships. However, it should not be forgotten that these sailing warships themselves were subject to a steady process of improvement which goes back into the 18th century, and indeed earlier.

From the beginning of the new century, spurred on by a combination of increasing timber shortage, and technical and industrial improvements, iron was used to an increasing extent in wooden ship construction. Iron knees replaced wooden ones, iron straps reinforced hulls, and iron chain was used to a greater extent in rigging. The great British shipwright, Seppings, besides engineering the changes noted above, also introduced a system of diagonal framing which made it possible to build much stronger and longer hulls than previously possible. Instead of just 200 feet, the practical hull length became 300 feet or more. As the maximum possible speed for a sailing ship (indeed any displacement hull) is a function of its waterline length, this was a step of great importance. Seppings, moreover, introduced stronger ways of building the ends of ships, which also gave better firepower at the bow and stern.

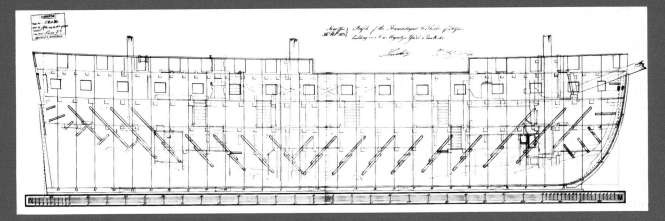

(above) This profile plan of the frigates *Hamadryad* and *Thisbe* shows Seppings diagonal riders which greatly increased the longitudinal strength of the hull, and also his round stern which made that end of the vessel much sturdier.

(below) This Admiralty plan of the large frigate *Raleigh* shows how the elliptical stern and round bow improved the field of fire of guns at the ends of a ship, besides making those ends less vulnerable to raking fire.

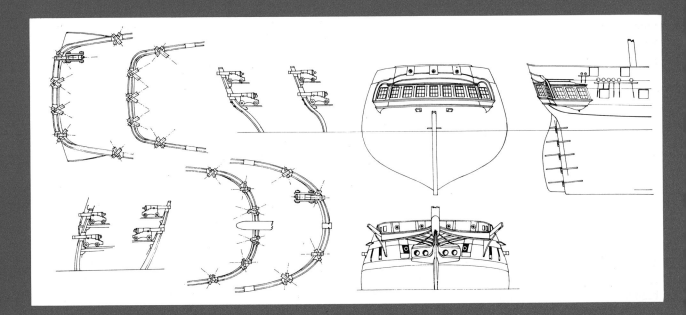

These developments had won general acceptance in the 1820's. Meanwhile, another improvement, this time a French one, was altering the conditions of naval warfare. Previously, the only missiles fired from naval cannon had been solid shot and various forms of anti-rigging and anti-personnel shot. The only explosive shells fired from ships had been projected from mortars during shore bombardments. Now, the French Colonel Paixhans developed the theory and practice of firing shells horizontally from large guns at another ship. The French Navy, rapidly followed by all the other naval powers, adopted shell guns with great speed. A shell, though lighter, and therefore with less penetrative power than a solid shot of the same size, could cause more damage to rigging and personnel, and greatly increased the risk of fire, always a danger in wooden ships.

The need for large cannon to fire shells contributed to an already existing tendency to increase the size of guns carried, and therefore to a much older trend, a steady increase in size of all classes of warship. To take an example, the standard frigate of the 1770's would have had an armament consisting of 12-pounders supplemented by 6-pounders. By the 1800's the main battery might be 18-, or even 24-pounders, with a powerful addition of short-range, but heavily shotted, carronades. By the 1820's the carronade had gone out of fashion as too short-ranged, but the main battery could be 32-pounders. By the 1830's small numbers of 68-pounders capable of firing 8-inch shells might be carried. These could be mounted on 'pivots' on the centre line at bow and stern, a development which first appeared on small gunboats in the late 18th century, but had spread to the largest vessels by this time.

As the size of guns increased, so the number carried for the same power and size of ship dropped. In effect, this meant that each warship type grew bigger and more powerful. For example, an 18-gun sloop of the 1830's was a more formidable proposition than, and the same size as, a small frigate of 50 years before. Even more obviously, the biggest frigates were encroaching on the preserves of the line of battleship. This process started with the Americans and Swedes in the 1790's and continued throughout the first half of the 19th century. These vessels retained the frigate characteristic of a continuous, gun-less, lower deck, but gradually abandoned the other characteristic, that of a single continuous gun deck. The quarter-decks and forecastles of the big 50- and 60-gun frigates were gradually turned into a single continuous 'spar deck'. This in effect meant that these ships had become 'two-deckers' (i.e. with two continuous gun decks) and therefore by previous definitions in the battleship class. Gradually the older types of sailing warship lost their prominence. The Royal Navy began no more 74-gun ships after the end of the Napoleonic Wars. Instead, the fleet was renewed with big two-decker 80's. These, with the three-decker 110's and 120's, were types made possible by the improvements in construction mentioned above.

As had been the case in the second half of the 18th century, various new types of hull shape were tried in an endeavour to improve performance. This was partly as a result of the alleged superiority of French sailing warship design (a complex and disputable question we do not have space to investigate here) and partly thanks to the 19th century obsession with speed. Unfortunately, the latter usually favoured extreme speed obtained in unrealistic conditions, often at the expense of real operational efficiency. A series of sailing trials by experimental squadrons publicised the matter but cannot be considered to be particularly effective for the scientific comparison of designs. Unfortunately for the Royal Navy the great Robert Seppings was replaced as the Surveyor of the Navy (i.e. chief designer, a post that would later be known as Director of Naval Construction) by a not particularly clever naval officer named Symonds in the early 1830's. The result was a series of vessels built with a characteristic 'peg top' hull form in section, copied from one used by both Americans and French to produce fast small ships. That it was a speedy hull form was undeniable; that it produced atrocious gun platforms, equally so. Designing sailing ship hull forms is an extremely complex business involving a great number of variables. There is little reason to believe that there was any real improvement in this aspect of sailing warship design in the 19th century.

The main externally visible difference in sailing warships between the late 18th and early 19th centuries was a tendency to reduce both external decoration and sheer (the difference in heights between the ends and middle of a deck). These were more matters of fashion than anything else, though the increasing number of larger flush-decked ships owed something to increasing concern with longitudinal strength.

The first steam warship, Fulton's *Demologus*, was produced for harbour defence. With her internal paddle wheel she was an original and interesting design, but one with no real influence on subsequent warship development. The first seagoing steam warships, the *Rising Star* for Chile (though she did have an internal paddle wheel) and the *Karteria* and her near-sisters for Greece, tended to a more conventional layout, as did the *Comet* of 1822, the Royal Navy's first successful steamship. It should perhaps be stated that the Royal Navy had a steam engine afloat (in a dredger) in the first year of the new century, and built an exploring steamer, which proved too weak to accommodate its intended engine, in 1814.

The *Demologus*, here given her alternative name of *Fulton the First*, is launched at New York in 1814, and the age of the steam warship begins. Though the contemporary caption calls her a 'steam frigate' this heavily-built vessel was designed for harbour defence, and would not have had the endurance or seaworthiness for operations on the high seas. The small schooner in the middle ground is firing her single central pivot gun in salute.

This dramatic print contrasts the two types of warship bought from abroad by the Greeks during their war for independence from the Sultan (1820's). In front is the paddle steamer *Karteria* (*Perseverance*) built in Britain and used to great effect by her British captain, Frank Abney Hastings, against Turkish shipping. The effect of red-hot shot heated in her boilers more than compensated the trouble her unreliable and weak engines gave. In the background is the large frigate *Hellas*, built in New York, and a fine example of the 'two-decker' frigates which were the pocket battleships of the day.

The *Comet* and the other steamers which followed her into service with the Royal Navy were fairly small vessels, usually armed with two or three guns, falling into the sloop category. They proved useful as tugs, despatch vessels and 'maids-of-all-work', particularly for river and inshore operations. Almost from the first, sailing ship hulls were converted to steam, first sloops and later frigates, to take advantage of the great number of incomplete hulls available.

By the 1830's the value of the steamship had been proved enough for it to be considered worth placing paddle engines, despite their known drawbacks, in frigates. In these developments the British, French and Americans kept more or less abreast of one another. By the end of the decade two new and crucial developments were causing admiralties to reconsider their building programmes.

The first to have a major effect was the introduction of the screw propeller. The invention of this device is disputed between several claimants, but there can be no doubt as to who were responsible for its general adoption. This honour is shared between the Swede John Ericcson and the Briton Petit Smith. The first-named, after a technically successful but otherwise fruitless trial in Britain, took his concept to America, where the *Princeton* was built, the first screw warship to enter service. At much the same time the Royal Navy was completing the *Rattler*, begun as a paddle sloop but rapidly converted to screw propulsion when the successful cruise of Petit Smith's experimental vessel *Archimedes* demonstrated the effectiveness of the new device. The extensive trials of the *Rattler* culminated in the famous tug-of-war with her paddle-wheel propelled sister, *Alecto*, in 1845. This was as much a public relations exercise as a scientific trial, for by this time the Royal Navy had already ordered several screw frigates. Even more important, in 1846, a ship of the line, the *Ajax*, went

to sea as the first screw battleship, and first steam capital ship, in the world.

At last steam could be applied to the largest warships. The screw was below the waterline and therefore not vulnerable to enemy action or the weather. Furthermore, it was easy to unclutch and hoist into a stern well so that it did not interfere with the sailing qualities of a ship. Engine and boilers were mainly under the waterline, and therefore protected from gunfire. There is small wonder that both Britain and France began a programme of putting engines into already existing ships of the line, and building new ones designed from the start

for steam propulsion. Perhaps the finest of these was the French *Le Napoleon* of 1850.

The Americans began building a number of very large screw frigates and corvettes. The main difference between the two types was no longer that the corvette was smaller, but that the corvette usually carried her guns on one flush deck, whilst the frigate, if not a 'two-decker', at least carried guns on two levels. This caused the British to build a series of six even larger screw frigates in the 1850's. These were designed by Baldwin Walker and were more powerful than any except the biggest battleships. The largest of these, the *Mersey* and *Orlando*, were 336 feet long, the longest wooden warships ever built, and they were armed with a main battery of 10-inch guns, heavier than any carried by ships of the line at that time.

Screw propulsion and wooden hulls were not an ideal combination. Wooden hulls were composed of many comparatively small pieces, thereby making the

The famous tug-of-war between paddle and screw in which the *Rattler* towed the *Alecto* backwards was followed by another less well-known repeat. Here, the screw sloop *Niger* defeats the paddle sloop *Basilisk*. It is obvious how much more of the former's side is available for the guns which were a warship's main reason for existing.

achievement of complete rigidity virtually impossible. Yet rigidity was vital to take the localised weight of the machinery, to resist the loosening effect of vibration, and above all to counter the torque of propeller shaft. Screw propulsion tended to shake wooden ships to pieces, and the almost inevitable distortion and flexibility of wooden hulls was bad for the efficiency of long, rigid drive-shafts which needed careful alignment to work at all. A further problem was that of making a watertight gland for the shaft to pass through. The adoption of new materials, particularly for the hull, provided the solution to these problems.

By the 1830's iron had been in use for some time for the hulls of small craft. However, there were difficulties in adopting it for seagoing ships. Not only were methods of producing large plates, girders and castings slow to develop, but also navigation depended so much on the magnetic compass that until some way of utilising this on an iron vessel was found the iron seagoing ship was unlikely to appear. In 1839 the Astronomer Royal, Airey, found a partial solution to the second problem and immediately iron warships were laid down. The first of these were built by Lairds of Birkenhead for the East India Company. These small gunboats were followed by a private venture paddle frigate, built in the hope that the Royal Navy would buy her. In the event the Mexicans purchased her instead, but shortly afterwards the Royal Navy did order a class of iron frigates. However, before these were completed a series of gunnery trials showed that the iron used in these vessels was liable to shatter very badly when struck by solid shot. The result was that they were hastily demoted to troopships. Two became famous in this role through the manner of their loss. The *Birkenhead* was wrecked in dramatic and heroic circumstances off South Africa (1852), whilst the *Megaera* had to be beached on a desert island to prevent her sinking from the effects of corrosion (1871).

The temporary abandonment of iron for warship hulls which lasted until the Crimean War, though it seems to us a retrograde step, made some sense at the time. Iron plates were often defective, and even the best appeared to be less able to stand up to shot than the thick planking and frames of a large wooden warship. Shellfire was less of a danger to a wooden ship with a well-trained crew than might seem to be the case at first sight. No major vessel had yet been destroyed by shellfire in action with other ships, though Danish warships had been set on fire and destroyed by Prussian field guns firing shells in 1849.

The outbreak of the Crimean War in 1854 makes a good point to stop and take stock of developments in the previous half-century. Ships had generally increased in size and gunpower, particularly with the addition of shell guns. All major navies had accepted

The *Agamemnon*, a screw line of battleship of 91 guns, launched in 1852. The funnel is well aft, indicating that the machinery is also as far back as possible to give a short propeller shaft and lessen the strain on the hull.

that, with the coming of the screw propeller, ships would be fought under steam. Major building and re-equipment programmes were fast approaching their aim of producing all-steam navies. Sail, however had not been replaced by steam as a method of propulsion when patrolling or making passages.

This is perhaps the best place to retail the later history of sail after it had been relegated to the status of a very necessary auxiliary method of propulsion. In the 1860's numerous warships intended for coastal defence or similar purposes, for which short-range was not a handicap, were built with steadying sails only. It was not until the 1880's that the ocean-going warship abandoned sail. This could happen then, thanks to a combination of the ever-increasing reliability of steam, the fuel economy of the triple-expansion engine, the world-wide spread of coaling stations, and, finally, the increasingly serious problem of the air resistance of masts, sails and rigging as speeds under steam grew. Vessels built for colonial police work and long-distance cruising often continued to be built with masts and sails till the end of the century, but these small cruisers, sloops and gun-

The first iron warship, *Nemesis*, proves her usefulness against some hapless Chinese war junks during the first Opium War. This small paddle-steamer had the shallow draft and agility to serve in the forefront in the river fighting of this war, unlike the sailing line of battleship which can be seen behind her bowsprit. *Nemesis* belonged to the Bombay Marine, the navy of the East India Company.

boats were of little technical or military importance.

Reverting to the 1850's, we see that two characteristic tendencies were already quite apparent. One was constant pressure to increase the size, power and expense of ships, which can be seen operating in a cyclical manner from the earliest days of the sailing broadside warship. A particular type of warship will increase in size as the years pass until it takes over the function of what used to be a bigger type. Meanwhile, this growth has created a gap which can only be filled by the development of a new smaller type, which will, in its turn, grow in size. We have already seen this happening with the frigate and sloop. Later, the torpedo boat would develop into the destroyer and thereby eventually create the gap which was to be filled by the appearance of the motor torpedo-boat.

The other tendency, partly due to the trend discussed above, was the increasing lack of satisfactory definitions of ship types. New technology and weapons were making it increasingly difficult to draw the old, fairly clear, lines between the different rates of ships of the line, frigates and sloops. The largest frigates were becoming as powerful as ships of the line, and though a distinct type, ought perhaps also to be considered as capital ships. This confusion of warship types, which has its parallels today, was to grow worse in the period which followed.

The first iron frigate, *Guadalupe*, built in the hope that the Royal Navy would buy her, but sold instead to Mexico. She was one of the protagonists in the extraordinary battle of Yucatan, where she, another paddler and several smaller vessels came off worse against two Texan brigs. Her heavy bow and stern pivot guns show up well in this print.

Ironclad to battleship

The Crimean War was to prove a decisive step in warship development. The frigate *Arethusa* became the last ship of the Royal Navy to go into action under sail alone, during the bombardment of Odessa. Rather more importantly, a superior Russian fleet gave a convincing demonstration of the destructive power of shellfire against Turkish ships at the so-called 'massacre of Sinope', which helped to bring Britain and France into the war. As soon as this happened the Russian fleet very wisely removed itself to its harbours to avoid a like fate. This meant that the allies' main naval task would be shore bombardment. This proved risky with wooden ships against shell-gun-armed forts. No major vessels were lost during the bombardments of Sebastopol, but there were some close shaves. It became increasingly evident that protection of some kind against shells was needed. Small gun boats built in large numbers was one answer, but the French came up with another solution: heavily armoured, shallow-draft steam 'floating batteries'.

Originally the French proposed to line the sloping sides of these box-like craft with cannon balls between two layers of planking. It was, apparently, a Briton who suggested that iron plates on a wooden backing was a better idea. The French rushed through the construction of a number of these monsters in time to use them in the successful bombardment of the fort at Kinburn. The British copied the French concept, though none of their batteries were complete in time to take part in the war. They

made one significant step, though, in building some of their craft with hulls, as well as armour, of iron.

This group of little known, ugly, slow and unseaworthy vessels were the first ironclads. The French ships at Kinburn, despite the many hits, suffered no serious damage to crew, guns or machinery. With wrought-iron armour ships could carry their guns close to an enemy with a fair degree of invulnerability. The potential of this for actions between ships (for which the floating batteries were not designed) was obvious and immense. The challenge to gunmakers to produce more powerful weapons capable of piercing the armour was equally obvious.

The success of these vessels led the French, under the guidance of their great naval architect, Dupuy de Lôme, to commence the building of seagoing ironclads. Invulnerable vessels of this kind would enable France to destroy British maritime preponderance at a stroke. The result was the *Gloire*, launched in 1859. De Lôme would have liked to build her entirely of iron, but given France's industrial state, and the need for speed in completion, this was not possible. Instead, the new ship had armoured sides on a wooden hull. Because of the weight of armour, and the heavy guns, she only had one main gun deck and was referred to as a frigate. This did not conceal the fact that she was the most powerful vessel of her day.

This happy state did not last long. The French were building a class of similar vessels, one of which, the *Couronne*, was to be iron-hulled, as well as a pair of two-decked ironclads with rams, the *Magenta* and

Solferino. The speed and volume of the British response was, however, overwhelming. In 1860 the first British ironclad was launched. Unlike the *Gloire* she was iron-hulled. She was also larger, faster and more heavily armed. Again, like the *Gloire*, the *Warrior* and her sister, *Black Prince,* were classed as frigates. In fact they, with the French ship, represent the only time a change in warship design has meant that all previous warships were totally outdated, useless and vulnerable. These vessels could have taken on the united navies of the world at the time of their construction without any risk of failure except through accident.

The early British and French ironclads represent a radical change in one sense, yet not in another.

Early steam warships had just added machinery to what was fundamentally a sailing ship hull. Now the ironclads added iron armour, and possibly an iron hull, with little else changed. Guns were still carried firing through ports in the sides and mounted on individual and fairly primitive carriages. The chief

The first seagoing ironclad, the French *Gloire*, looks much less impressive than the two-decker screw battleship behind her stern, particularly as the latter has a much more extensive rig. However, the *Gloire* could destroy her with ease, and without sustaining any serious damage. The *Gloire*'s rig shows an intermediate stage in the reduction of sail to an auxiliary. There are two small coast defence steam gunboats in the bottom right-hand corner of the picture, forerunners of the later and larger 'flatirons'.

visual difference was that most ironclads had a ram bow. The broadside ships which followed the *Warrior* down British slipways were modified in a few small features, the chief difference being a tendency in the later vessels towards reduced length for increased manoeuvrability and decreased cost.

The impressive British answer to the *Gloire*. This is the *Black Prince*, the second of the 'black snakes of the Channel Fleet'. She has long since been broken up but her predecessor and sister, *Warrior*, is still in existence as an oil jetty at Pembroke Dock. She was the first British battleship, and the last afloat. At the time of writing the Maritime Trust is working towards her restoration and preservation, both for her importance in warship history, and because of her significance as one of the most important and complex industrial products of the 19th century.

The original idea of protection in an ironclad was merely to run a belt of armour all, or at least most of the way, around the sides of a ship. This was practicable with the original thicknesses of armour used. However, almost immediately the race between guns and armour began. Heavier guns had to be carried behind thicker plating, which necessarily restricted the area of side that could be armoured. One main theme which can be traced behind the somewhat bewildering variety of ironclad types built between 1860 and 1890 is the problem of finding the best way of mounting and protecting heavy guns in ships. Three main approaches to this problem appeared in the 1860's. The first was to mount the guns inside a rotating turret, a circular box of armour rotating on

rollers or a spindle. This was developed simultaneously by Ericcson in the USA and by Coles in Britain, though the latter's proved the better design. Alternatively, the armour could be concentrated on a 'box battery' or 'citadel' amidships, a sort of armoured fort in the middle of the ship. Inside this the guns could usually be moved from one fixed gun port to another by means of a complicated system of rails known as 'racers'. The French developed the third alternative, the 'barbette'. This was an armoured tower protecting the gun machinery and ammunition hoists. The guns were mounted on a turntable over this. In some ships various combinations and permutations of these three methods were tried.

Each device had its own advantages and disadvantages. Turrets, because of their weight, had to be mounted low in a ship, and therefore produced low freeboard and consequently poor seaworthiness. On the other hand, they gave their guns a wide field of fire, and therefore greater flexibility and economy in numbers of guns than a broadside or box battery vessel. Conversely, the box battery allowed a comparatively high freeboard, but restricted the field of individual weapons. In broadside fire only half or less of the guns could be used against a given target. The barbette, like the box battery, permitted a high mounting, and therefore good freeboard. However, the guns themselves and their crews were not protected, or at least not well sheltered from hostile fire.

The turret, because of its requirement for low freeboard, was at first restricted to ships intended for coastal use. The first British ships of this type, the *Royal Sovereign* and *Prince Albert*, completed in 1864 and 1866, respectively, were both very interesting ships, in many ways ahead of their time, but little noticed either then or later. The first was a conversion of a wooden ship of the line, cut down nearly to the waterline, and the second was purpose-built and iron-hulled. Both had no more than steadying sails, since they were intended for coastal defence, and both had four turrets on the centre line. In the case of the *Royal Sovereign* the forward turret held two guns. This gun layout was not to be repeated until the Dreadnought period.

More spectacular, if less lasting, developments diverted attention to the other side of the Atlantic. Ironclads had been considered in the USA as early as the 1840's, and in 1854 money was actually allocated to building one. This was the 'Stevens Battery', a vessel in advance of both its time and the nation's ability to build such a ship. The design was of extreme and probably excessive ingenuity, featuring twin screws, guns mounted on turntables above a central citadel, a flooding system to reduce the target area in action, internal sloping armour and an ambitiously high speed. It is usually a mistake to try to put too many new ideas into one ship, especially when the industrial resources available were barely adequate for building more conventional

(left) This photograph of *Benbow* fitting out shows her forward barbette, and her massive 16.25-inch, 110-ton gun in the loading position. She was the only ship of the 'Admiral' class to have this huge weapon, though two were also carried on the *Victoria* and *Sans Pareil*. The gun was in advance of technology because it tended to droop at the muzzle, and had a very short effective life. The legs and hoisting block in the foreground belong to a pair of sheer legs, a device for hoisting heavy weights into ships.

(right) The first British box battery ship fires at the first British turret ship. *Bellerophon* conducts gunnery trials to test the strength of *Royal Sovereign*'s turrets in 1866. They suffered little damage and were still in working order after three hits. The lowered bulwarks of the turret ship emphasise her low freeboard compared with the fully-rigged *Bellerophon*.

iron ships. The result was that the Stevens vessel was never completed, though the project lingered on into the 1870's.

American industry could not cope with such a complex design, but when war came between the North and South in 1861, both sides showed great ingenuity in improvising warship designs. The Confederacy, with very little industry, was forced to the greater degree of improvisation. Having captured the partially-burnt hull of the frigate *Merrimac* at Norfolk Navy Yard, an armoured battery was built above the waterline, using railway iron and similar in shape to the Crimean floating batteries. An iron ram was added to the bow, and the vessel, though handicapped by unreliable engines, sallied forth under the name of *Virginia* to deal with the Federal fleet in Hampton Roads. The destruction caused by this apparently invulnerable ironclad, and the arrival a day later of the *Monitor*, with the ensuing indecisive duel, is one of the classic tales of naval warfare.

The *Monitor* and her successors were a somewhat more sophisticated answer to the problem of producing ironclads in the shortest possible time. They were basically the smallest and lowest possible craft capable of carrying one (or in some cases two) Ericcson turrets, with two of the largest possible smooth bore guns inside, up to 15 inch in calibre. The traditional 'cheesebox on a raft' description is a good one. The deck and waterline armoured belt projected beyond the edges of the wooden hull. Freeboard, crew comfort and seaworthiness were minimal. However, they were very useful for inshore work, particularly bombardment. The *Monitor* herself showed her vulnerability to bad weather by foundering off Cape Hatteras, where her wreck was found recently. Besides the 'monitors', the turreted vessels named after their prototype, the North also built a much more sophisticated form of the floating battery type of vessel, which was all the South could

attempt. This was the *New Ironsides*, a ship which was as superior to the hastily improvised (and mostly never completed) Southern ironclad fleet as she was inferior to the more powerful European ironclads.

For a short while after the American Civil War there was a 'craze' for monitors, and both Russians and Swedes built numbers of copies. However, even for coastal defence, the British and French preferred to build vessels with rather more seaworthiness and superstructure. British private yards had already constructed much more seaworthy vessels equipped with one or two Coles turrets. These were placed behind dismountable bulwarks, and the vessels had raised forecastles and poops and were equipped with masts and sails. They lacked the all-round fire of the American type of turret ship, but were much more versatile. Most were fitted for ramming, and two, ostensibly built for Egypt, became a *cause célèbre* as the 'Laird Rams', being actually intended for the Confederacy. They were finally purchased by the Royal Navy as the *Scorpion* and *Wivern*. The experiences of the *Rolf Krake*, built for Denmark, and later the *Huascar*, built for Peru, showed the value of these comparatively small vessels in action.

To obtain the necessary seaworthiness for an ocean-going battleship, and the space for the requisite masts and sails, it was vital to place turrets well away from the ends of a ship. This was done in the first pair of major seagoing turret vessels built for the Royal Navy at the end of the 1860's. The *Monarch* proved a satisfactory ship. Unfortunately, Captain Coles objected to features of her design and, after much public controversy, was allowed to design a vessel to his own ideas. The unfortunate *Captain*, with a low freeboard made lower by the failure to control the weights put on board during construction, provided an object lesson in the importance of leaving ship design to professional naval architects by capsizing in the Atlantic, taking most of her crew and her designer with her.

Meanwhile the Royal Navy had a class of small 'breastwork monitors' built for colonial defence. These had low ends, two turrets mounted at either end of a raised platform, or 'breastwork', amidships, and no more than steadying sails. These were in many ways the prototypes of the battleships which followed twenty years later. One, *Cerberus*, in very dilapidated form, survives as a breakwater in Australia, though there are now plans to preserve her.

For more than two decades from the 1860's there was great enthusiasm for the ram as a primary weapon. A concomitant was a shift of emphasis from broadside to end-on fire, which would be a useful supplement to the ram during the approach and necessary manoeuvring at close quarters before ramming. The seagoing turret ironclad, with the high forecastle and poop masking end-on fire by turrets on the centre line, was modified by placing the usual pair of turrets *en echelon*, offset on either side of the ship, a layout seen in such massive ships as the Italian *Dandolo* and HMS *Inflexible*.

The alternative was to omit the raised ends and the masting, thereby producing a larger version of the small 'breastwork monitors', and removing any obstacle to bow and stern fire. Compound engines meant that the range of the 'mastless battleship' was now adequate for more than coastal defence. The

This print of the breastwork monitor *Cyclops* gives a very good impression of the breastwork on which the two turrets and central superstructure are mounted. She was completed in 1877 for coastal defence. She spent her life in home waters, but sisters were built for colonial defence, and one of these, the *Cerberus*, survives in Australia.

The seagoing turret battleship *Colossus*. Her main armament is in the two turrets *en echelon* amidships. Though laid down in 1879, she was not completed until 1886, one of the victims of the 'dark ages' of the Navy. Though in most respects a smaller version of the great *Inflexible*, she and her sister *Edinburgh* were the first ships to revert to breech-loading guns. The exiguous nature of the rig by this time on even a fully seagoing battleship is evident in this picture.

only major handicap that remained with the *Devastation*, the first of these vessels, which entered service in 1873, was that her low freeboard made her very wet in anything but calm weather. This handicap still applied to the last British battleship fitted with true turrets, the *Hood* of 1893, and was the major reason why turrets were replaced by other means of gun protection.

The other major British answer to the problem of mounting heavy guns, the box battery, first appeared in the mid-1860's in ships such as the *Bellerophon*. She was also the first British battleship designed specifically for ramming, and was much shorter, broader, and more manoeuverable than her predecessors. The introduction of the balanced rudder helped with the latter quality, particularly as it was not until a little later that power steering was generally adopted.

The need for end-on fire was partially met by recessing the ship's sides in the way of the corners of the battery, thereby enabling a port to be cut pointing towards bow or stern or, alternatively, a couple of guns could be 'sponsoned out', with part of the battery projecting beyond the sides. Much the same effect could be obtained by giving a pronounced inward slope ('tumble home') to the sides at either end, but this feature was more often used by the French with their side-mounted barbettes.

The box battery was obsolete by the 1880's, for it was basically an uneconomical and ineffective way of carrying guns when compared with rotating mountings. The future lay with the barbette. The French had introduced this, though an interesting variant was tried in the 'great brig' *Temeraire*. In this case the bow and stern barbette guns were actually lowered within the mounting for reloading. This 'disappearing mount' worked, but was extremely heavy, complex and expensive. The first true barbette ship built for the Royal Navy was the *Collingwood*

laid down in 1880 and completed in 1887. With this ship, and the following and similar 'Admiral' class the true battleship emerged from the ironclad. With comparatively high freeboard, the unprecedentedly high speed (for a battleship) of 16 knots, a battery of 6-inch and 6-pounder guns amidships and the combination of waterline belt and sloping armoured deck for protection, the *Collingwood* is quite clearly the direct predecessor of the type of warship later known as 'pre-dreadnought'. It is somewhat of a surprise to find that she was followed by a reversion to turret ships, particularly the massive, ugly and much less effective *Sans Pareil* and *Victoria*. It was not until the 1890's that the *Royal Sovereign* class clearly established the pre-dreadnought pattern.

One of the most important features of the *Collingwood* was that she marked the point at which the Royal Navy finally adopted the breech-loading gun. Up to the late 1850's all naval guns had been muzzle-loading smooth bores, plus a few, largely experimental, weapons with some form of rifling. This gave the projectiles greater accuracy by spin-stabilisation, and also permitted elongated shells with consequently greater explosive capacity, to be fired. Starting in 1858 the Royal Navy took the bold step of re-equipping with the new Armstrong gun, which was breech-loading as well as being rifled. The idea of breech-loading had been known and used as far back as the 15th century, and in theory it allowed more rapid and convenient loading. However, it needed a good deal of precision engineering to make the seal of a movable breech gas-tight against the enormous pressures developed within the bore. Though the Armstrong at first seemed to have solved this problem satisfactorily, experience, especially at the bombardment of Kagoshima in Japan (1863), showed that the breech of the Armstrong was unreliable. The answer to this was to revert to muzzle-loading, but to retain rifling and elongated shells.

The new guns were not made by the old methods of casting and then boring out from solid. Instead they were 'built up' of tubes shrunk on top of one another, a technique which permitted the manufacture of much larger and stronger guns. This meant that higher velocities could be obtained for piercing the increasing thicknesses of armour being used. Gun size increased from 9 to 12 inch calibre, then to the massive 16 inch in the *Inflexible* and the huge, almost unfireable 17.7 inch which Armstrongs' persuaded the Italians to fit in the *Dandolo* and *Duilio*.

It would not have been possible to work such big guns without the development of hydraulic machinery for moving and loading them. The *Inflexible* was fitted with a loading system which rammed the charges and projectiles into the muzzles from outside the turrets, when the guns were lowered into recesses below a sloping deck ('glacis'). The remains of a similar system can still be seen by the coastal defence turret surviving on the pier just outside Dover Marine Station.

The French and Germans had found more effective methods of breech-loading by the 1870's, but the Royal Navy remained committed to RMLs (Rifled muzzle loaders) until the end of the decade. With the 1880's came the changes in types of explosive which were to revolutionize gunnery. The new chemical industry replaced the black powder (gunpowder) that had been standard with, first, prismatic powder, then nitro-cellulose (gun cotton), followed by cordite. The use of these slower and more accurately burning propellants meant that both the length and the range of guns could be greatly increased. There were teething troubles, several

This photograph of *Anson* in a seaway shows how the low freeboard forward of the 'Admiral' class handicapped them at sea.

ships being lost from spontaneous combustion in their magazines, before experience taught the best ways of keeping explosives safe. Perhaps the most famous accident of this kind was the one which caused the loss of the *Maine*. This was blamed on sabotage and offered the pretext for the Spanish-American War. At much the same time as the change in explosives, gun construction was improved by the introduction of wire-winding. Wire wound round the inner-tube of the gun gave greater strength than the old built-up method. Though this new type of gun was generally adopted in Britain, the Germans and others continued to use improved forms of built-up guns.

Improvements in guns were sooner or later matched by better armour. At first the main improvement was in the thickness of wrought iron used. In the fifteen years between the *Warrior* and *Inflexible* the width of the belt grew from $4\frac{1}{2}$ to 24 inches. Such an increase necessarily meant a corresponding reduction in the area covered by the armour, from virtually the entire side of the ship to the limited area of a central citadel enclosing machinery and magazines but little else. The unarmoured ends had to be increasingly subdivided against the danger of enemy fire concentrating there and causing uncontrolled flooding. The use of steel armour temporarily eased the situation by enabling thinner plates to be used for the same protective effect. The main problem was finding the right balance between hardness and toughness. Hard steel was better at preventing a shell penetrating, but, thanks to its greater brittleness, was more liable to crack. The answer was to use a combination of hard and softer metal. This was first achieved by using composite armour, a steel face on wrought iron backing. This was not, however, ideal, as experience showed it was liable to flake under the impact of projectiles. The American process of 'Harveyising' steel, treating the face to make it harder than the rest of the plate, won general acceptance in the 1880's, only to be replaced by the end of the century by the similar but more effective German Krupp method. By this time more powerful guns were enforcing a steady increase in the width of armour again.

To revert to the development of the battleship, the period of confusion of types and methods of mounting guns, which made for small numbers of experimental vessels built slowly, was brought to an end by the construction in Britain in the early 1890's of the large class of *Royal Sovereigns*. This impressive class, completed in an unprecedentedly short time combined all the innovatory features which had marked the *Collingwood* with much greater freeboard. At last

A painting of the British Channel Squadron, about the end of the century. In the foreground are light cruisers, in the middle are the heavy cruisers, and beyond the line of battleships which would appear to be *Royal Sovereigns*. The high freeboard of these vessels is obvious when compared with earlier turret and barbette ships.

the really seaworthy 'mastless' battleship was a
reality. The main armament was still mounted on top
of barbettes, and had to be loaded by training on to
the centre line, and lowering the breeches into holes
in the back of the barbette. This method was shortly
to be replaced, first by covering the guns and the top
of the barbette with an armoured hood, then by
developing methods which permitted all-round
loading. The first innovation was adopted in the
smaller *Renown* class which followed the *Royal
Sovereigns*, and was improved in the large and
numerous *Majestic* class, which also adopted the
second development. In this last class the 12-inch
gun became the standard heavy armament and
remained so for the next decade. In effect the

armoured hood was no more than a turret mounted
on top of the barbette, and the word 'turret' soon
came to mean this type of mounting. The French
had already begun to adopt a somewhat similar
expedient, but with rather more resemblance to the
old circular turrets.

The excellent series of battleship designs which
followed the *Royal Sovereign* into service with the
Royal Navy, and which were the responsibility of the
great Director of Naval Construction, Sir William
White, set the pattern for most foreign construction
as well for the decade which ended with the *Dreadnought*. A twin heavy gun mounting beyond either
end of a central superstructure incorporating heavy
secondary and tertiary gun batteries, two funnels,

and a generally well-balanced silhouette, became the norm at this time. The secondary battery, at first usually of 6-inch guns and later increasing to 8 or 9.2 inch, was intended as a useful supplement to the main armament in the comparatively short ranges expected in battle. There were some who felt that the much greater rapidity of fire from the smaller guns would be of greater value than the heavier but fewer shells of the big guns. Obviously the more shells that were fired, the greater was the chance of a hit. However, the experience of the Russo-Japanese War showed that the smaller weapons were of comparatively little use against armoured targets. This, combined with the need for salvo firing and effective fire control created by the much greater ranges

possible with the new explosives, were the factors that led to the construction of the 'all big gun' ship of which the *Dreadnought* was first. The tertiary battery of 6- and later 12-pounder guns (designated by the weight rather than the size of the projectile they fired, unlike bigger weapons) was intended chiefly for use against torpedo craft.

With improvements in machinery the range and speed of battleships steadily increased. With the later pre-dreadnoughts speeds had reached 18 knots, but clearly there was little potential for growth left in the marine reciprocating engine. The adoption of the turbine in the *Dreadnought* was to prove at least as important an innovation as her gunnery arrangements.

This photograph of the French battleship *Jaureguiberry* at speed shows to advantage the characteristic features of large French warships of the last decade of the 19th century (she was completed in 1896, and was therefore a contemporary of the British *Majestics*). The 305-mm guns at either end, the 274-mm on the sponson amidships and the twin 138.6-mm at each corner of the superstructure are all in small round turrets. The midships sponson shows up the great tumble-home of the sides. The massive 'military masts' complete the 'fierce face' aspect, so beloved of French designers at that time.

The tools of empire

Small sailing warships were usually just smaller versions of their larger contemporaries, the only fundamental difference between a sloop and a line of battle ship being in size. The smaller ships tended to have proportionally faster lines and less gun-carrying power, and might possibly be optimised for service in shallow water. The smallest vessels, cutters, schooners, brigs and luggers, would also differ in rig, but still carried guns on the broadside in a wooden hull fundamentally similar to that of a larger vessel. Basically they were unspecialised vessels, though they were intended for different purposes than the larger vessels, which were the only ones capable of fighting in the line of battle. The smaller craft were used for cruising warfare, scouting, convoy escort and coastal work. However, a larger vessel could be used for these purposes as well and it is symptomatic that at the beginning of the 19th century 'cruiser' did not mean a special type of warship but merely any type of fighting ship on detached cruising service. The only exceptions to the lack of specialisation at this period were the purpose-built shore bombardment ships (bomb vessels), the fast-disappearing fireship type (many of which were also purpose-built in the 18th century), and the rowing gunboats for inshore use.

This situation remained much the same during the first half of the 19th century, altered only by the fitting of steam engines in sloops and frigates, and, as we have seen, by a gradual blurring of distinctions and functions inherent in a general increase in size.

However, the second half of the century saw the evolution of various specialised types. Those associated with torpedo warfare will be dealt with in the next chapter. What concerns us here is the development of the gunboat, and the slow evolution of different types of cruiser.

The appearance of the ironclad immediately introduced a sharp line of demarcation between ships which were armoured and those which were not. Initially even very small ships were given the full ironclad treatment, and the Royal Navy built a small number of ironclad sloops during the 1860's. These did not prove particularly satisfactory. The ships that continued to be built for the traditional cruising tasks of trade protection, commerce raiding and scouting were frigates, corvettes and sloops of the old type. They had screw propulsion, full rig, sometimes with guns on the centre line working from pivots on the centre line, but still firing through ports on the broadside, but basically still the direct descendants of their sailing predecessors.

The ships which were so successful as commerce raiders for the Confederacy, *Alabama*, *Shenandoah*, and their sisters, were very much in this tradition. One factor that all the successful raiders had in common was that they did not have iron hulls. Experience showed that iron tended to foul very rapidly with growths of weed and other marine life, thus greatly reducing speed. Until comparatively effective anti-fouling paints were developed towards the end of the century, iron hulls were not suitable for ships that had to spend long periods at sea, particularly in the tropics. The first answer evolved was composite construction. Instead of using iron in small pieces in the construction of a wooden hull, as had been done early in the century, the entire frame or skeleton of the ship was made in this material. This was then planked with wood, on top of which copper sheathing could be fixed. Coppering, the most effective protection against fouling known at the time, could not be applied direct to iron because of the disastrous electrolytic corrosion that would result. Composite-built ships began to appear in the late 1850's. It is worth noting that true composite construction was not, as is so often stated, an intermediate stage between wood and iron shipbuilding, but a reaction to the early shortcomings of iron. The main drawback was that composite construction was much more expensive than iron, so later another solution was found, sheathing the bottom of an iron ship's hull with wood, and then putting copper over this. 'Wood sheathing' remained a feature of ships intended for service on distant stations until the end of the century.

The beginning of the true cruiser probably came with the ending of the American Civil War. The Americans, very conscious of the possibility of war with Britain and the consequent value of very large, fast and powerful raiders, had begun building a group of these. The *Wampanoag*, the first of these, was intended for a speed of 17 knots. She made this speed on trials, but only at the cost of wrecking her engines and straining her hull. Her design was over-ambitious for the resources available. In particular, too much was attempted with a wooden hull. However, the fear of such large, powerful and speedy ships loose against British commerce prompted the building of a vessel big, strong and fast enough to counter this menace. This was the origin of the *Inconstant*. She was followed by other large un-

armoured cruisers such as the *Shah*, but the experiences of this ship in trying to cope with the *Huascar*, where her lack of armour prevented her closing to a decisive range, seemed to show that so large a vessel ought to have some form of protection. Numbers of ironclads were built whose light armour and other attributes put them in the cruiser rather than the battleship category. An example was the *Imperieuse* of 1886, the only British warship to have her four guns in the diamond-shaped layout more common with French ships. Most of these ships, however, were lacking in speed.

They counted as 'armoured cruisers', a type whose first example was the Russian *General Admiral* of 1874. She was answered by the *Shannon* of 1877, the first to rely for part of her protection on a horizontal armoured deck added to the hitherto prevalent belt. Later, many cruisers relied solely on such a deck, which usually sloped to offer vertical as well as horizontal protection. The deck would cover the vitals of a ship, the machinery and magazines. This type of cruiser was known as a 'protected cruiser': only those cruisers with vertical side armour were 'armoured'.

In the mid-1880's the Royal Navy completed the *Orlando* class which had a very narrow belt that was completely submerged when the ships were fully loaded! For the next few years the Royal Navy built only protected cruisers. Armoured cruisers re-appeared a decade later in Britain. However, the *Orlandos* also made a positive contribution to development by establishing what was for long to be the standard layout of the larger cruisers, with 9.2-inch guns mounted fore and aft and a broadside of lighter guns. In effect, these vessels were more lightly protected, less heavily gunned and faster versions of the battleships of the day. They were not necessarily smaller than battleships, for ships such as HMS *Powerful* or the French *Jeanne d'Arc* were considerably longer and had more powerful machinery than their battleship contemporaries.

The French became particularly enthusiastic about building big armoured cruisers for commerce raiding. These would be capable of sinking anything as fast, and running away from anything more powerful. The first of these was the *Dupuy De Lôme* of 1890. She had an armour belt covering the entire length of the hull and was the first warship with triple screws. This became a standard propulsive layout in the

The French armoured cruiser *Dupuy De Lôme*, showing her extraordinary ram bow. This proved a very unseaworthy feature. Her design was influential when it first appeared (launched in 1890) but she ended her days sold to Peru, the later French armoured cruisers were of a less extreme shape.

French Navy, and the Germans followed suit, but the Royal Navy stuck to twin screws, and, when later more power was needed, quadruple screws.

Twin screws had been common for warships from the 1860's. The extra manoeuvrability and reliability of two shafts instead of one, together, in some cases, with the reduced draft made possible by such an arrangement, counterbalanced the extra complexity and expense. This was not the case with merchant ships, which for some time, with a few specialist exceptions, remained devoted to single shaft propulsion.

The massive British protected cruisers of the mid-1890's, *Powerful* and *Terrible*, the largest warships of their day, were built because of rumours of a power-

ful new Russian ship. They were a classic case of over-reaction, as the ship they were designed against proved to be much less impressive than was at first thought. This affords an obvious illustration of the futility of attempting to design vessels to counter specific foreign ships. There are very few cases in naval history of such intended rivals meeting each other in action. It makes far more sense to follow the more normal British practice of designing ships to fulfil particular tasks and requirements, such as the traditional cruiser's purpose of trade protection.

The development of the heavy cruiser (though this term was not used at the time) kept pace with battleship design. It was to culminate in the 'Dreadnought armoured cruisers' *Invincible* and her sisters, which were later to be renamed 'battlecruisers', where the fundamental error of combining a battleship armament with cruiser protection was made.

The Royal Navy, with its pressing requirements for trade protection and imperial policing, built large numbers of medium-sized cruisers, whose largest guns were normally of 6 inch calibre. The 'C' class vessels, classed as corvettes when built in the late 1870's, were of this type of ship, as were the *Mersey*

This photograph of the protected cruiser *Terrible* at sea shows just how large this ship, and her sister *Powerful*, were. She has the four funnels and relatively small superstructure typical of the larger British cruisers of the period around 1900. The two heaviest guns are mounted in turrets on bow and stern. All the others are in casemates sponsoned out of the side of the hull.

One of the most famous episodes of seamanship in the 19th century. The 'C' class corvette *Calliope* battles her way out of the lagoon at Apiah during the Samoa hurricane. A series of freak events made the lagoon a death trap during this storm, and all the other warships there, American like the ship in the background whose crew are cheering the British ship on, and German, were wrecked. Only the *Calliope* survived, thanks to a lucky position, good engines, and the skill and devotion of her engineers and captain. Ships had to be designed to fight the sea as well as other enemies.

class of the 1880's and the *Highflyers* which came into service with the new century. In the late 1880's some dissatisfaction with this type was caused by the Armstrong firm building the *Esmeralda* for Chile. She packed an armament and protection more appropriate to a large cruiser into a hull of moderate dimensions. This was done at the expense of less visible qualities such as endurance, seaworthiness, and ammunition supply, but she successfully established a vogue for 'Elswick cruisers' (named after the Armstrong shipyard where they were built) amongst the navies of the world. Most of the subsequent ships of this kind were better balanced designs and less overloaded than the *Esmeralda*, which the Chileans soon sold to Japan.

Small cruisers were also built in numbers for service on distant stations, and it is often difficult to see where the line of distinction between this type of warship and the sloop is to be drawn. They were normally smaller versions of the bigger cruisers of the day, though tending to be more conservative in appearance, especially in keeping sails for longer. Of rather more interest are the beginnings of the light cruiser. This was a type of vessel designed for scouting, and usually intended for use in home waters. The despatch vessel *Iris* of 1879 is perhaps the first example of the type. She was a graceful, yacht-like ship, and the first major naval vessel built entirely of steel. Much earlier, the French had used some steel in one of their first ironclads, and torpedo-boats were built of steel from the start. However, it was not until the Siemens method of producing mild steel appeared in 1876 that it was possible to supply steel of the quantity and quality required for ships of any size at an economical price. Once the *Iris* had shown the way, the obvious advantages of steel in strength and lightness enabled it to replace iron in virtually all new construction in a very short time. It is worth noting that, for mainly economic reasons,

this transformation occurred rather later with merchant ships.

The Germans played an important part in the evolution of the light cruiser. They gradually evolved a tough, seaworthy and well-armed series of designs, intended for fighting in the North Sea, from small torpedo ships of the torpedo gunboat type. These culminated in the long series of classes named after cities, built in the early years of the 20th century. The Royal Navy, though it had built torpedo cruisers in the mid-1880's, did not pursue this line of development with any consistency until after our period ends.

Most of the smaller ships used for policing work in distant waters, sloops, gunboats, gun vessels and the like, were of little technical interest, being merely smaller versions of the older type of cruiser, and usually keeping sails to the end of our period. It is worth noting, however, that most of the real work of the navies of the time, the gunboat diplomacy, and most of the action, fell to these ships and the cruisers. The battle fleet served its purpose by existing, and by showing itself in cruises and exercises. Had there been a major maritime war the same would probably have applied for most of the time. This was certainly the case in the closing years of the Napoleonic Wars, when the frigates and sloops did most of the work of exploiting the sea control won by the ships of the line in battle and blockade.

One type that does deserve mention is the 'Crimean gunboat'. The Crimean War produced an urgent requirement for small shallow draft steamers capable of carrying one or more big guns for shore bombardment, relying on smallness, numbers and agility for survival. A very large flotilla of these craft was built for the war, and modified and enlarged versions proved very useful for inshore work in the more remote parts of the world after the war had ended. In a way these could be considered a replacement for the bomb vessels, none of which were built after 1830, and all of which were out of service long before 1854. However, the need for high-angle fire was not satisfied by the gunboats, and a large class of mortar barges was built. Rather surprisingly, no attempt was made to provide any other high-angle fire vessels for the rest of the century, except by the Americans who used mortar schooners and barges during their Civil War.

A completely different form of gunboat was built in some numbers in the 1870's. This was the 'flatiron' or 'Rendel' gunboat, intended for coastal defence rather than offence, for anti-ship work rather than shore bombardment. The principle behind these was to fit the largest possible gun into the smallest possible hull. Twin screws were fitted for shallow draft and manoeuvrability as the fixed gun was aimed by pointing the ship in the required direction. These were basically descendants of the rowing gunboats which were still in service early in the century, and were also an alternative to torpedo-boats, presenting much the same appeal of a cheap, potent and small weapons system. For a while there were those who maintained that these vessels rendered the battleship

The Crimean gunboat *Magnet*. The figures of her crew show how small she is. Her heaviest gun is visible just abaft her mainmast. She is a simple, indeed basic, vessel.

obsolete, as, theoretically, large numbers should have been able to overwhelm a battleship. This was very similar to the intermittently repeated assertion that the battleship was outdated by the torpedo-boat. The latter idea had slightly more justification, but neither proved true. No navy of any strength at this time could do without battleships, though the French, under the influence of the *Jeune École*, tried to do so for a while. The battleship was too powerful and too capable to be ignored, even if it was no longer completely invulnerable to all except another of its own kind. In the event, the 'flatirons' proved very unseaworthy and far too vulnerable to other small vessels armed with light guns. They were only a passing fashion.

In the second half of the century, for the first time, specialised types were developed for river warfare. The great struggle on the rivers of the Mississippi system during the American Civil War produced some hastily improvised, but fascinating, designs. Eads built a series of battery ironclads powered by a semi-enclosed sternwheel which proved vital to the North's victory in this area. One has recently been salved and preserved. Other vessels ranged from 'cottonclads', ordinary river steamers given a gun protected by bales of cotton to a sternwheel turret ironclad.

The exploitation of Africa, Asia and South America was largely effected along the lines of the rivers, and specialised river gunboats proved very useful. The

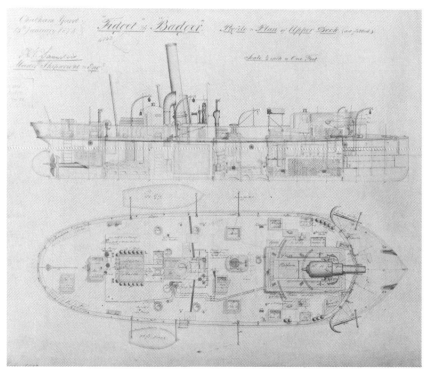

(left) The 'flatiron' gunboats *Fidget* and *Badger* are shown in this Admiralty plan. They are small shallow draft vessels built round the great 10-inch gun.

(right) Sternwheel gunboat of the *Tamai* class, designed by Yarrow and built by Elder's (later Fairfield) for service on the Nile. They were built for the unsuccessful expedition to relieve Gordon at Khartoum in the Sudan (1884–5), and played a useful part over a decade later in Kitchener's reconquest of the Sudan. The main weapon is a small muzzle-loading gun, supplemented by Nordenfelt machine-guns, for which a choice of mountings is provided. This plan comes from the builder's collection at the National Maritime Museum.

main problem was usually achieving extreme shallow draft. This usually meant adopting either paddles or twin screws. For very shallow rivers, particularly narrow ones, sternwheelers were normally preferred. From the 1870's an alternative was developed by the British firm of Thornycroft, and refined by their great rivals, Yarrow. This was the expedient of partially enclosing the propellers in raised tunnels within the hull, reducing both the draft and the danger of damage to the propellers. The 'tunnel screw' river steamer was faster and more efficient than the sternwheeler, but also more expensive, and more difficult to run or repair. These extreme-shallow-draft vessels were usually shipped out in pieces to be assembled at their destination. This sometimes involved carrying the individual pieces on the backs, or heads, of native porters, which restricted the dimensions and weight.

The British-built Russian sternwheel gunboat *Aral*, for service on the inland sea of the same name. She may stand as a representative of the hundreds of small warships built in British yards for foreign navies.

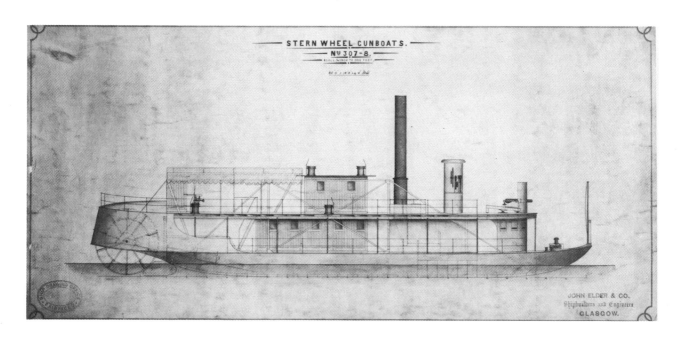

The underwater threat

The submerged mine first became a regular feature of naval warfare during the Crimean War. The Americans had used 'infernal machines' during both the War of Independence and the War of 1812. The British had attacked Napoleon's invasion flotilla in its ports by swimmers using explosives, but it was the moored contact mines which damaged a couple of small British ships in the Baltic which really began the era when warship designers had to take the threat of underwater attack into account.

Making a hole below the waterline of a ship is by far the most effective way of sinking it. An explosion underwater, in close contact with the hull, is a particularly good way of making such a hole, as the incompressibility of water ensures that the effect of the explosion is concentrated against the hull. Not only is water let in, which may sink the ship, but also the explosion may set off the magazines, or disable the machinery. These, the most vulnerable parts of a ship, are mostly below the waterline.

The problem for the attacker was to bring the explosive charge against the enemy's hull. Mines (originally, and confusingly, known as 'torpedoes') relied on enemy ships steaming up to them, and therefore were chiefly of use for protecting entrances to harbours, rivers, or for coastal defence. The Americans had used drifting mines during the War of Independence, but this was a technique that could only be used in special circumstances, and was dangerously indiscriminate. The years which followed the Crimean War saw progressive improvements in moored mines. 'Observation mines' laid defensively across a waterway could be set off by electricity from a shore station. The most effective variety of the more versatile 'contact mine', set off by the impact of a ship hitting it, was developed by the Germans in the 1870's with the 'Herz horn' which, when broken, set off an explosion by means of a chemical reaction

A model of the *Royal Sovereign*, the name ship of her class of classic pre-dreadnoughts, the first of a successful series of British battleships with high freeboard, barbette mountings, and a powerful secondary battery. Later classes placed the twin funnels abaft one another instead of side by side, and the big guns were given armoured hoods ('turrets') but the basic layout remained the same until the *Dreadnought* revolutionized battleship design.

producing an electrical impulse. Other less efficient but still workable methods were used, notably by the Confederates, who improvised moored mines as well as ones mounted on stakes. These weapons achieved the first sinkings of ships by mines, one of which produced Farragut's immortal 'damn the torpedoes' as he continued to attack despite the loss of one of his ships. However, it was the Russo-Japanese War which really established the mine as a major weapon. Battleships were lost to mines on both sides.

Mines could be laid by any ship or boat. Though some small steamers were built for coastal use in laying defensive minefields, no specialised offensive minelayers were built until just before the First World War. The main effect of mines on ship design before this was to encourage the increasing sub-division of hulls into watertight compartments, and the adoption of double bottoms. These developments limited the effect of underwater damage, and became even more important as the potentialities of two other forms of underwater attack came to dominate naval thought.

The first was the revival of the old galley-warfare tactic of ramming. This was used to some effect during the American Civil War, but more influential was the sinking of the Italian *Re d'Italia* at the battle of Lissa in 1866 by the ram of the Austrian *Ferdinand Max*. The Italian ship was stopped at the time. Such incompetence could not be relied on in an opponent, but for some twenty years thereafter the idea of ramming dominated naval tactics and had much influence on ship design. Most large warships and many small ones were given protruding and reinforced rams. Many vessels were designed to be short and highly manoeuvrable to use this weapon to the best effect. As late as 1890 the Royal Navy was building a class of cruisers designed especially for ramming. Earlier, many warships were referred to as 'rams', an indication that this weapon was given

The beginning of mine warfare. The small British warship *Merlin* is damaged by a Russian 'Infernal Machine'. Both the mine and the damage to ship's side are shown in this Admiralty plan. A similar mine was recovered intact and now is on exhibition at the National Maritime Museum.

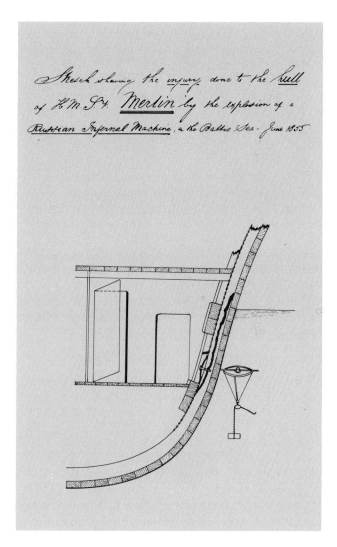

equal importance to their guns. As an example one can count the 'turret rams' *Scorpion* and *Wivern*.

Some vessels were built with the ram as their primary weapon, as a group perhaps the most useless warships ever designed. The first was the diminutive tug *Manassas* converted by the Confederates, with a low cigar-shaped hull and a single gun in the bow. The French *Taureau* class were much bigger vessels but with much the same appearance. Astonishingly, the Americans launched the *Katahdin* in 1892, with the ram as her only effective weapon, and that quite useless because of the low speed and lack of manoeuvrability of this vessel. The best of the group was the British fast and manoeuvrable *Polyphemus*, but she was not really a ram, as we shall see.

By 1890 not only was the improvement in guns and gunnery such that the chance of getting close enough to use the ram was reduced nearly to vanishing point, it had become very obvious that it was extremely difficult to ram another vessel which

The reinforced ram of the *Sans Pareil*, seen just before her launch. A similar ram, that of the *Camperdown*, sank the *Sans Pareil*'s sister, the *Victoria*.

was under way and determined not to be rammed. A number of vessels were sunk by ramming in the late 19th century, but nearly all were lost in peacetime accidents, most notably the celebrated case of the *Camperdown* sinking the *Victoria* during squadron manoeuvres (1893).

Not only were ships lost during the American Civil War by ramming and mining, it was also the conflict when torpedo-boats made their first successful attacks. Fulton seems to have been the first to propose underwater attack by explosive projectiles at the beginning of the century, but he proposed firing these from submerged cannon – not a very practicable idea. The much simpler device of fixing a shell or specially prepared charge on the end of a long pole run out over the bow of a small steam boat was adopted by both sides during the Civil War. It was used by Lieutenant Cushing in a ship's steamboat in his attack against the Confederate ironclad *Albemarle*. The attack was a success, and Cushing survived, though when the 'spar torpedo' exploded it swamped the boat and put out the fire in the boiler.

The Confederates adopted the new weapon with enthusiasm. They improvised special vessels for carrying it, the semi-submersible steam-powered 'Davids' and the *Hunley*, the man-powered submarine. The latter carried out the first successful submarine attack, against the *Houstatonic*, but was herself lost with all her crew as a result of the explosion. Fast steam launches were built in Liverpool to carry spar torpedoes for the Confederacy, though it does not appear that they were ever completed.

The spar torpedo was not quite as suicidal a weapon as appears at first sight. The force of the explosion was concentrated on the target's hull and usually did not endanger the attacking boat. The device was chiefly intended for surprise attacks,

This plan of a steamship's boat shows her armed with spar torpedo, dropping gear for Whitehead torpedoes, a quick-firing gun and a machine-gun, weapons which altered fighting techniques and ship design during the latter part of the century. Sturdy wooden-built boats like this proved much more satisfactory for carrying on board ship than the purpose-built but fragile second class torpedo-boats

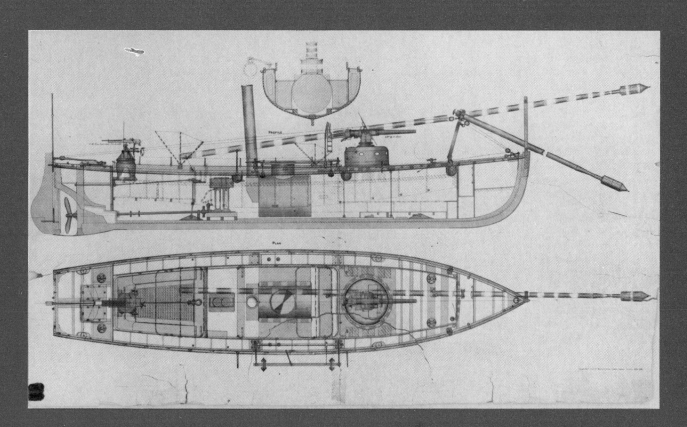

usually by night, using stealth and small size for concealment, which explains the ability of the 'Davids' to submerge until only funnel and conning tower were visible. Once detected, high speed and manoeuvrability were important for completing the attack and for the getaway. It should be remembered that the big guns of the time were slow firing and could only be traversed and elevated slowly, so small fast vessels were in little danger even at point blank range. The rifles of the crew of the target vessel were probably the worst menace.

The US Navy built a number of large and unusual spar torpedo vessels immediately after the end of the Civil War, but these had little influence. It was not until the early 1870's that the first true torpedo-boats appeared. These were the products of two British firms which had specialised in the construction of small fast river launches with light steel hulls and light powerful machinery. Both firms were the creations of inventive young men, John I. Thornycroft and Alfred Yarrow, who built their first launches with their own hands (though the 16-year-old Thornycroft was helped by a younger sister!). Thornycroft built what is usually accepted as the first torpedo-boat in 1870 for the Norwegian Navy. This vessel, capable of carrying spar torpedoes and having a speed of 18 knots, was called the *Rapp*, and is still in existence. She had the unusual feature of being able to use another type of torpedo as well, a 'towing torpedo' towed from the top of the funnel. During the 1870's several forms of towing torpedo saw service in several navies, but this explosive equivalent of the later paravane was more of a menace to squadron-mates than the enemy, and faded from the scene fairly rapidly.

The development that made the torpedo-boat into one of the most important types of vessel of the late 19th century was the invention of the 'locomotive' or 'fish' torpedo. The original idea of the Austrian

soldier, Luppis, was for a wire-guided, clockwork-powered explosive boat. During a long series of practical trials during the 1860's, the *emigré* English engineer Robert Whitehead, working at Fiume (now Rijeka in Yugoslavia), developed it out of all recognition. By the time the Royal Navy tried the new device it was a submerged missile with a warhead of guncotton, powered by compressed air, and guided by a hydrostatic device (Whitehead's 'secret') which kept the weapon at a set depth. At this stage range was a maximum of 600 yards, and speed somewhere around 6 knots. These performance figures would steadily improve with time, as did warhead capacity and accuracy. For the first time a very small vessel had the potentiality of sinking a much larger one at a distance. Various other methods of propulsion and guidance were tried in the following years. Electric and wire-guided torpedoes were invented, and for a time at the end of the century the US Navy was equipped with the flywheel-driven Sims torpedo, but it was the steadily-improving 'Whitehead' which defeated all rivals.

In the early 1870's the question which agitated the major navies was how to utilise this promising new weapon. The Royal Navy appointed a Committee in 1873, which produced a prescient report. It suggested four different ways of carrying the torpedo into action. One was on board already existing warship types, and by the end of the decade most battleships and cruiser-type warships were fitted with some kind of torpedo-launching gear. The second was to use ships' boats, the third was to build special seagoing torpedo ships, and finally the possibility of using small, fast, purpose-built steam launches was mentioned.

To take the third suggestion first, the Royal Navy was already building an experimental torpedo vessel. This was the *Vesuvius*. She was a comparatively slow (9 knots), small vessel designed with a submerged bow torpedo tube, and intended for attack by surprise and stealth. Her silhouette was low, her engines intended for quiet operation, and her boilers fired by smokeless coke. It was intended to get rid of the exhaust gases through side ducts, though she was completed with a more conventional funnel. From the first she was used for experiments and training. No similar vessels followed, but she was an intelligent design for the time, and might well have proved

more effective in wartime than the extremely fragile early torpedo-boats. As it was, she survived to be the last torpedo-boat in the Royal Navy, not being broken up until the mid-1920's.

Her design was enlarged and altered out of all recognition in the far larger faster and more powerful *Polyphemus* which entered service in the early 1880's. This vessel is often thought of as a ram designed to fit the theories of the aged Admiral Sartorius. This is a complete misconception, as the account of her designer (Nathaniel Barnaby) and other official papers show very clearly. She was, in fact, intended from the start as an armoured torpedo ship, with a powerful submerged battery of torpedo tubes and reloads. The ram was only fitted as a secondary

The torpedo ram *Polyphemus* charges the boom at Berehaven at full speed (1885). This episode which took place during exercises was the high point of her existence and culminated in scattering the fragments of the broken boom in all directions. This view emphasises the low, almost submarine-like silhouette of this powerful vessel.

weapon, and in case the side-firing submerged tubes (for which she was the trials vessel) did not work properly. As it was, a long period of trials proved the concept of these tubes, and they were widely fitted in large warships from then on. Often derided as a 'freak', the *Polyphemus* made a great deal of sense as a fighting ship at the time of her conception. With her 3-inch armoured sloping deck, her high speed of 17 knots, and her powerful battery of five torpedo tubes, she would have proved a very dangerous opponent to contemporary battleships. It was the introduction of quicker-firing, and, perhaps even more important, quicker-traversing guns which made the concept less attractive, and probably explains why no similar vessels were built, as these developments occurred at much the same time as she was entering service.

A number of 'torpedo cruisers' were built in the early 1880's, but they proved rather small and unseaworthy, and it was found simpler to fit more conventional cruisers with torpedo tubes. Thereafter, for a while, the specialised seagoing torpedo vessel faded from the scene. However, it might be considered that, with the torpedo gunboat, the increasing size of the torpedo-boat, and especially the growing size of the destroyer, the steady growth of the smaller types of torpedo craft had recreated the seagoing torpedo vessel by evolutionary development.

Ships steamboats were often fitted with dropping gear for 'Whiteheads' and also spar torpedoes. Some were used for torpedo attacks as late as the 1914–18 War. In the late 1870's and early 1880's numbers of 'second class' torpedo-boats were built, designed to be small enough to be lowered from ships' davits and be faster than the ordinary boats. These were particularly popular with the Royal Navy, conscious of the difficulty of forcing smaller navies to fight, and therefore welcoming vessels which could attack the enemy in his bases. For a while the Russians in-

creased the enthusiasm for such craft by successful operations against the Turks using torpedo-boats carried in ships to near the enemy coast. This spurred both British and French to build special torpedo-boat carriers, which also served as depôt ships. The first Royal Navy vessel was the merchantman *Hecla*, purchased and converted for the rôle. Later, the cruiser-like *Vulcan* was specially built. She can almost be considered as an ancestor of the aircraft carrier, with her six second-class boats carried ready for launching. However, these boats proved very fragile, and in the long run slower but sturdier ships' boats built of wood rather than thin steel took their place.

The characteristic torpedo-carrier of the late 19th century was the torpedo-boat proper ('first class t.b.'). It proved easy enough to fit Thornycroft and Yarrow spar torpedo-boats with torpedo-dropping gear or tubes instead. From the start the chief consideration was speed, though speed obtained in the unrealistic circumstances of smooth water, lightly laden trials with expert crews. This speed would bear little resemblance to the much lower figure obtained after a few years' service, in rough water, and with ordinary naval crews. Probably in no other respect, except the story of the popularity of the ram, does late 19th-century ship design seem to us to depart so far from what would appear to be sensible. This was the fault of the lack of any real operational experience. It is true that seagoing experience slowly enforced a steady increase in the size of torpedo-boats. This was, however, as much due to the need for more machinery to make the boats go even faster as it was to enable them to operate in less sheltered waters.

The *Lightning* of 1876 was the Royal Navy's first torpedo-boat; 80 feet long with a speed of some 18 knots. It is interesting to note that she was originally intended by her builder, Thornycroft, to have an early variant of the hovercraft principle, air lubrication of the hull. The technical limitations of the day were enough to prevent such a futuristic step.

By the mid-1880's, 125-feet long boats capable of over 20 knots were being built, and by the 1890's lengths of 150 feet and speeds of 25 knots were common. With the increase of size went more powerful armament; light guns were added, torpedo

sizes rose from 14 inch to 18 inch diameter, and the numbers of tubes increased from one to, in some cases, five. For a while, torpedo-boats seemed, to many naval theorists – and to many of the enthusiastic young officers who commanded them, to have doomed the battleship. The French were particularly keen, as they saw these boats as a means of nullifying British naval predominance. They built up a very large torpedo force, as did the Russians, which in turn forced the Royal Navy to devote much effort to devising defences against the torpedo-boat.

One defence against these small vessels has left its mark on the coasts of Europe, in the form of the vast breakwaters which surround harbours such as Portland or Cherbourg. These are less defences against the sea than preventive measures against surprise torpedo attack. Vessels could create their

The *Lightning*. A builder's plan showing the Royal Navy's first torpedo-boat. The bow tube was added about a year after completion. Previously, torpedoes had been carried in dropping gear at the sides. Two reloads for the tube could be stowed on the deck rails. The characteristic shape of the locomotive boiler, and the odd Thornycroft divided rudder with the screw behind it, show up clearly.

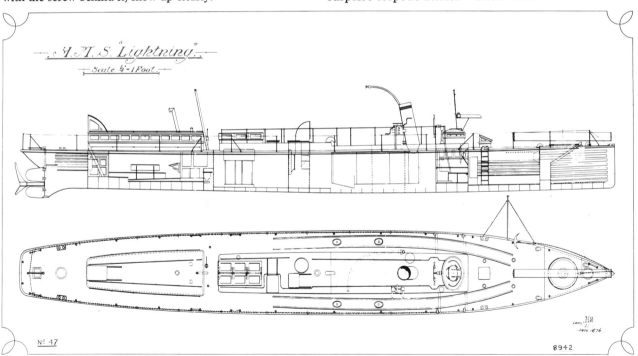

In the foreground of this photograph, taken about 1880, is a row of Russian torpedo-boats of the *Lightning* type with bow torpedo tubes. They have been hauled up on blocks to save their fragile hulls from harm. The nearest has a split rudder, with the shaft passing between the two halves, and the propeller behind the rudder, a feature which was also seen in early Thornycroft steam launches.

The extraordinary craft in the background is a 'Popoffka', a circular coastal defence vessel, with her guns mounted in the centre. It was one answer to the problem of restricting the area to be protected, but the attendant problems of powering and steering this monstrosity proved too great for more than two to be built. These were the *Admiral Popov* and the *Novgorod*, the latter of which is seen here.

own portable defences by using net barriers slung around the hull, but these, though fitted to large ships from the 1880's, were really only of use when at anchor. They could be used under way but heavily restricted speed and manoeuvrability. The importance of detecting night attacks led to the rapid adoption of the new electric light in the form of searchlights. The two most effective defences, however, were the newly developed quick firing gun, and small fast vessels designed for use against torpedo-boats.

Machine guns had been used in the American Civil War, and were widely adopted by navies for close-quarter fighting and anti-personnel work. Initially, the Nordenfelt, Hotchkiss, Gardner and Gatling guns used for this task were the worst menace that the lightly-plated torpedo-boats had to face. By the beginning of the 1880's the fitting of recoil cylinders and more efficient central pivot or pedestal mountings to progressively larger sizes of gun produced 3- and 6-pounders, and later 3-, 4-, and even 4.7- and 6-inch 'quick-firers'. These, with their high rate of fire and rapid gun-laying, made very effective anti-torpedo-boat weapons. As a side effect, the need to carry numbers of such weapons led inevitably to an increase in the size of larger warships. The torpedo threat also increased the need for internal subdivision to prevent flooding, and thereby produced a further addition to the size of battleships.

The principle of setting a thief to catch a thief begins very early in the story of the torpedo-boat. Nearly every increase in the size of British torpedo-boats was heralded by the claim that the new vessels, fitted with more light guns in the place of torpedo tubes, would be effective counters to their foreign equivalents. The '125 footers' of 1886 were even ordered as 'torpedo-boat destroyers'. Torpedo-boat builders produced a number of designs of their own for enlarged torpedo-boats intended for just this

purpose, for example, White's *Swift* which became the Royal Navy's TB 81.

Another approach was tried with the 'torpedo gunboats' or 'catchers' which were built in some numbers for the Royal and other navies in the late 1880's and early 1890's. These were basically very small light cruisers with the emphasis on torpedo and light gun armament. They proved a very qualified success at best. They were too slow to catch torpedo-boats in good weather, and not seaworthy enough to accompany the fleet in really bad weather. They would probably have proved adequate escorts to the British fleet in most circumstances (which should have been their real purpose) but few paused to consider this, thanks to the prevailing obsession with speed. Their slowness was due to difficulties with their boilers, which merit digression.

Larger ships had for long used fire tube boilers of the type usually called 'scotch'; reliable but heavy and relatively inefficient. Torpedo-boats used 'locomotive' boilers, similar, as the name suggests, to those used for railway engines. These were lighter and more efficient, but required skilled stoking and management to give the best results. They also proved, when used in the TGBs, to be unsuitable for larger vessels. The answer proved to be to use water tube boilers, in which the water was carried through the hot gases of the firebox in tubes instead of vice-versa. These were eventually to prove far more efficient and lighter than their rivals, but they suffered from a fair share of teething troubles. There were also a variety of different designs to choose from. The result was that the 'battle of the boilers' raged with considerable controversy in the late 1880's and early 1890's, until the water tube boiler in a developed form emerged the clear winner. One factor that helped in this outcome was that the only TGB fitted with water tube boilers, Thornycrofts' *Speedy*, proved to be by far the best of the type.

In place of the TGB the torpedo-boat destroyer was to emerge as the nemesis of the smaller craft. In 1893, the two chief British torpedo-boat builders (who had been suggesting such a development for some time), under the direction of Admiral Sir John Fisher (then Controller of the Navy), produced the designs for the first TBDs (the title was soon shortened to 'destroyer'). Thornycroft (whose rôle has usually been neglected) and Yarrow each built

a pair of the new vessels to their own designs, rapidly followed by another two built by Laird. *Havock*, *Hornet*, *Daring* and *Decoy* were merely enlarged, up-gunned and faster torpedo-boats. The increase in scale, however, made them far more effective than their predecessors, and as they carried torpedoes as well as guns, they could not only destroy, but also replace, torpedo-boats. These pioneer vessels were designed for 26 knots, but in view of the excellent trials results of the Thornycroft boats, the large numbers of similar vessels ordered to counter the French torpedo-boat threat were to be '27 knotters'. In view of higher speeds obtained by new French torpedo-boats the even larger class of slightly enlarged destroyers building in the late 1890's were '30 knotters'. The quest for absolute speed was taken even further with three experimental vessels intended for 33 knots, though none reached that speed.

At the end of the century sanity returned, and the next group of destroyers, the 'River' class, were enlarged, intended for a sea (as opposed to trial) speed of 26 knots, and fitted with a raised forecastle instead of the earlier 'turtle back' bow, in order to permit higher speed and to keep them drier in rough weather. A less developed form of the raised forecastle had already proved very effective in a class of German torpedo-boats. The Germans had a particularly efficient torpedo-boat arm, and had already built enlarged vessels as division leaders, though as they were more concerned with using the torpedo than with developing the destroyer function, their armament was not altered from that of the conventional German torpedo-boats.

The River class were more heavily and strongly built than earlier destroyers, and in many ways can be considered as more successful descendants of the TGBs than as a direct continuation of the torpedo-boat line of development. With them the destroyer came of age.

A dramatic photograph of one of the 27-knot destroyers, the *Janus*. This emphasises her small size and narrowness. Her biggest gun, a 12-pounder, is mounted on the same platform that serves as her bridge, only protected by canvas screens. Most of her length is devoted to boilers and machinery.

Conclusion

In some ways the situation at the beginning of the 20th century resembled that 100 years before. In both cases there was a firmly-established hierachy of warship types, for the confusing turmoil of experiment and uncertain purpose of the previous 50 years had finally produced the clearly separated types of battleship, cruiser (large and small) and destroyer. However, the early 20th century was to see the pace of development increased to an even higher level than before. The great increases in battleship size and power of the Dreadnought era were beginning. These would be mirrored in the development of the lesser types of warship. Already the turbine was offering great improvements in engine performance. The French had submarines in service which could be considered to be practical, if somewhat limited, weapons of war rather than potentially useful experiments. The outbreak of the First World War would soon establish this type of vessel as the most successful torpedo-boat of all. In 1903 the Wright Brothers flew at Kitty Hawk, and the aircraft, even more than the submarine, would revolutionize both the methods of naval war and warships themselves.

Weaponry was undergoing similar dramatic developments. New explosives had produced vastly increased potential ranges for guns, and the pioneering work in fire control of the Briton, Percy Scott, and the American, Sims, with others, was making the potential into reality. This development might have relegated torpedoes to a minor rôle, had not two developments increased their speed, range and accuracy in a similar manner. Obry's development of gyroscopic guidance produced far greater accuracy, and permitted proper advantage to be taken of the slightly later development of 'heated air' torpedoes. This meant that the compressed air in torpedoes was used to support the burning of fuel, and the products of this combustion then powered the engine, thereby greatly increasing power and therefore speed and range.

These dramatic technical developments could be exploited immediately they appeared because the intense national rivalries of the beginning of the 20th century greatly reduced budgetary restraints on shipbuilding. These had been very tight indeed earlier in our period, particularly in the 1870's and early 1880's. The size, performance and fighting power of ships had been restricted by arbitrary limitations imposed on grounds of economy. It is interesting to wonder how much this factor delayed technical advance. Financial restrictions on shipbuilding have always been a feature of naval history, but never has the situation in modern times been so severe as in the period of Gladstone.

One innovation which has not been mentioned so far, but was of great importance in the last part of the 19th century, was the development of the science of hydrodynamics, and more especially the techniques of tank-testing of models. The leader in this field was William Froude, who began advising the British Admiralty on hull shapes in the 1870's, and then set up a testing tank at Alverstoke with Admiralty backing. This institution played a very important part in the evolution of hull design, and nearly all Royal Naval vessels of the last quarter of the century had their lines tested there.

It would be wrong to complete an account of warship design without some mention of the men who served on board the ships. Conditions of life on board improved between the beginning and the end of the period. Improved methods of food preservation (refrigeration was introduced on board larger warships by the end of the century), the use of electric light and of steam and other forms of heating, all made for better conditions. However, it is worth noting that the technical improvement of the introduction of the iron hull meant a temporary setback in living conditions. Iron hulls sweated, and provided little insulation against extremes of temperature, and ventilation problems were worse. In the end these defects were remedied by new developments such as improved ventilation devices, insulation, and heating arrangements.

The technical changes meant great changes in the seamens' way of life. No longer was the emphasis on agility aloft, the case of rope and canvas, and the use of manpower for virtually all tasks. Instead, an increasing need was felt for technical knowledge and mechanical ability. The days of the seamen as a combination of traditional craftsman, trained acrobat and human donkey engine were fading and being replaced by those of the seaman as a machine minder. These changes took a long time to work out, and indeed are not completely achieved even now. They had their social repercussions, which were equally slowly worked out. One of the most fascinating stories of the 19th-century navy is the climb of the engineer from an unwanted and despised hired hand, to slow acceptance as an officer living in the wardroom. This slow ascent is a fine symbol of the basic change of the 19th-century warship from a wind-driven wooden vessel operated by traditional skills, to a much more complex entity, metal-hulled, driven by steam, to which new devices were added with increasing frequency, and which required considerable technical and even scientific knowledge from her crew.

An end and a beginning. The *Hibernia*, one of the penultimate class of pre-dreadnoughts, with a Short seaplane ready to take off from a platform on her bow on a trolley. Lieutenant Sansom achieved this feat when the ship was steaming at 10½ knots, in May 1912. The ship shows the addition of 9.2-inch guns in turrets at the corner of the superstructure to the 12- and 6-inch guns of the earlier pre-dreadnoughts. She was one of the *King Edward VII* Class, nicknamed the 'Wobbly 8', as there were eight ships in the class, and their steering was notoriously erratic.

Acknowledgements and select bibliography

This work owes much to the experience of working for years on the immense collections of plans and associated documents on ship design at the National Maritime Museum, particularly the Admiralty Collection. I am equally, if not more, indebted to conversation and correspondence over the years with the following friends and fellow researchers: Paul Akerman, Philip Annis, Basil Bathe, David K.Brown, John Campbell, Norman Friedman, Robert Gardiner, Ian Grant, Steve Kirby, Brian Lavery, Hugh Lyon, Christopher Morris, George Osbon, Alan Pearsall, Antony Preston, Alan Raven, the late John Saltmarsh, Dave Sambrook, Roderick Stewart, Len Tucker, Piet van der Merwe and many others to whom I apologise for not naming. Particular thanks are due to the General Editor of the Series and to Michael Dandridge for their help in the preparation of this work. To all of them goes the credit for any merit this work may have. Mine is the responsibility for mistakes and inadequacies.

The coverage of the history of the warship during this period in published works is very patchy, particularly for the earlier half century. These are a few of the more useful works available in English:

Parkes, O. *British Battleships* London 1957

Chapelle, H.I. *History of the American Sailing Navy* New York

Preston, A. and Major, J. *Send a Gunboat!* London 1967

Hovgaard, W. *Modern History of Warships* (reprint) London 1971

Baxter, J.P. *Introduction of the Ironclad Warship* Harvard 1933

Hansen, H.J. *Ships of the German Fleets* New York 1975

Wilson *Ironclads in Action* London 1896

Kennedy, P. *The Rise and Fall of British Naval Mastery* London 1976

Fincham, J. *History of Marine Architecture* London 1851

Albion, R.G. *Forests and Seapower* Harvard 1926

Bartlett, C.J. *Great Britain and Seapower 1815–1853* Oxford 1963

Marder, A.J. *Anatomy of British Seapower* London 1940

US Navy *Dictionary of American Fighting Ships* Washington 1959 onwards (several volumes)

Articles in the *Mariners Mirror* (especially by Admiral Ballard and G.Osbon,

Articles in *Warship* (especially by D.K.Brown)

Articles in *Warship International*

Articles in *American Neptune*

Foreign language works that are particularly useful include H. Le Masson's work on French torpedo-boats, the excellent series of official histories of Italian warship types published by the Naval Historical Office at Rome, and Groener's *Die Deutsche Kriegschiffe*.

Further suggestions for reading will be found in Albion's bibliography: *Naval and Maritime History* (David & Charles, 4th edition, Newton Abbot 1973).

Index

THE SHIP

The first four titles in this major series of ten books on the development of the ship are: 2. *Long Ships and Round Ships: Warfare and Trade in the Mediterranean, 3000 BC–500 AD*, by John Morrison; 5. *Steam Tramps and Cargo Liners: 1850–1950*, by Robin Craig; 8. *Steam, Steel and Torpedoes: The Warship in the 19th Century*, by David Lyon; and 9. *Dreadnought to Nuclear Submarine*, by Antony Preston.

The remaining six books, which are to be published 1980–1981, will cover: 1. Ships in the ancient world outside the Mediterranean and in the medieval world in Europe (to the 15th century), by Sean McGrail; 3. The ship, from *c.*1550–*c.*1700 (including Mediterranean, Arab World, China, America); 4. The ship from *c.*1700–*c.*1820 (including Mediterranean, Arab World, China, America), both by Alan McGowan; 6. Merchant Steamships (passenger vessels), 1850–1970, by John Maber; 7. Merchant Sail of the 19th Century, by Basil Greenhill; and 10. The Revolution in Merchant Shipping, 1950–1980, by Ewan Corlett.

All titles in *The Ship* series are available from:

HER MAJESTY'S STATIONERY OFFICE
Government Bookshops
49 High Holborn, London WC1V 6HB
13a Castle Street, Edinburgh EH2 3AR
41 The Hayes, Cardiff CF1 1JW
Brazennose Street, Manchester M60 8AS
Southey House, Wine Street, Bristol BS1 2BQ
258 Broad Street, Birmingham B1 2HE
80 Chichester Street, Belfast BT1 4JY
Government publications are also available through booksellers

The full range of Museum publications is displayed and sold at
National Maritime Museum
Greenwich

Obtainable in the United States of America from Pendragon House Inc.
2595 East Bayshore Road
Palo Alto
California 94303

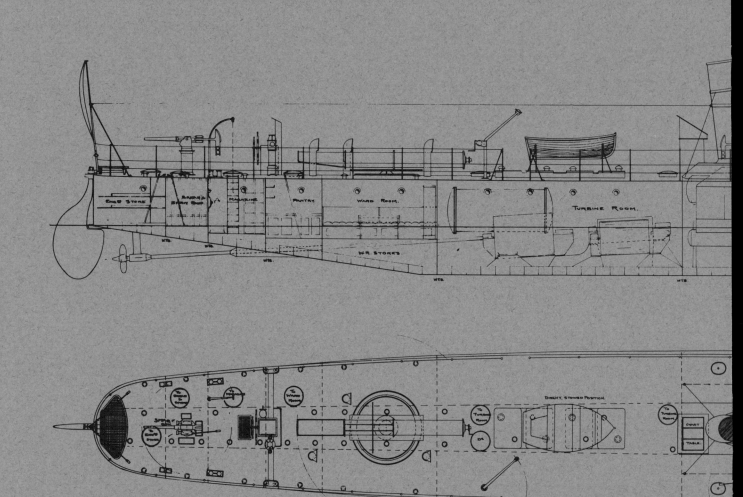

ENGS STORE   ENGINEER'S ENGINE ROOM   MAGAZINE   PANTRY   WARD ROOM.   TURBINE ROOM.

W.R. STORES.

W.T.B.   W.T.B.   W.T.B.   W.T.B.   W.T.B.

DINGHY, STOWED POSITION.

TO TURBINE ROOM   TO WARD ROOM   TO TURBINE ROOM   CHART TABLE.